Praise for GOD'S TROPHY WOMEN

"Jacqueline Jakes has the best kind of wisdom—the kind that is earned by triumphing through experiences that turn a test into a glorifying testimony. If you are finally ready for victory over the battles of your life, GOD'S TROPHY WOMEN is your divinely inspired guide."

—Valorie Burton, author of
What's Really Holding You Back?
and *Listen to Your Life*

"In this book, Lady Jacqueline has uncovered a great hidden treasure chest, full of much needed medicine for the soul. There is healing for those who can't even say where it hurts. There is a breakthrough for those who may not even claim to be bound. Most of all, there is a wonderful revelation of *whose* we are, in spite of *who* we are. Thank you, Jacqueline! Thank You, Jesus!"

—Dr. Rita L. Twiggs, preacher,
teacher, author, and one of
God's Trophy Women

Praise for Jacqueline Jakes

"Offers insight and wisdom of the ages to help women find balance in a quick-fix, fast-paced world."

—*Essence*

"Keep this book [*Sister Wit*] by the side of your bed—the more you read it, the more it will become a treasured friend."

—*Gospel Today*

"[*Sister Wit*] is a fine, richly textured garment that will comfort readers' hearts."

—*Charisma*

"Telling her story with honesty, punctuated by Scripture and humor, Jakes opens up her life and heart."

—*Library Journal*

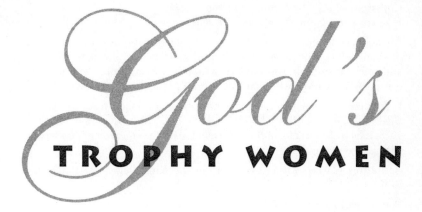

God's TROPHY WOMEN

You Are Blessed and Highly Favored

JACQUELINE JAKES

Foreword by T. D. Jakes

WARNER
Faith®

New York Boston Nashville

Unless otherwise noted, Scripture quotations are taken from the HOLY BIBLE, NEW INTERNATIONAL VERSION®. NIV®. Copyright © 1973, 1978, 1984 by International Bible Society. Used by permission of Zondervan. All rights reserved.

Scriptures marked KJV are taken from the King James Version of the Bible.

Warner Faith

Time Warner Book Group
1271 Avenue of the Americas, New York, NY 10020
Visit our Web site at www.twbookmark.com

Warner Faith® and the Warner Faith logo are trademarks of Time Warner Book Group Inc.

Printed in the United States of America

First Edition: May 2006
10 9 8 7 6 5 4 3 2 1

Library of Congress Cataloging-in-Publication Data

Jakes, Jacqueline.
  God's trophy women : you are blessed and highly favored / Jacqueline Jakes. — 1st ed.
       p.   cm.
  Summary: "Stories of women who have triumphed through their faith in Jesus Christ. Some are women of the Bible; some are the seemingly ordinary women who fill our lives." — Provided by the publisher.
  Includes bibliographical references.
  ISBN-13: 978-0-446-57782-3
  ISBN-10: 0-446-57782-0
  1. Women in Christianity — Biography. 2. Women in the Bible — Biography. I. Title.
  BR1713.J35   2006
  248.8'43 — dc22   2005032885

Book Design and composition Nancy Singer Olaguera/ISPN

*This book is dedicated to the memory of three powerful
women in my life: My mother, the late Mrs. Odith P. Jakes,
and my two grandmothers,
Mrs. Susie W. Patton and Mrs. Lorena Gray.
I am blessed to have witnessed, in both sides of my family,
however briefly, women who were strong, courageous, successful,
and triumphant believers in the Lord Jesus Christ.
These were women who made a difference in the lives of others,
and this world is left better from their being here.*

ACKNOWLEDGMENTS

There are so many to acknowledge when writing a book. A myriad of people have encouraged me and offered prayers and hope for the completion of the project.

The people who readily come to my mind are: my baby brother, T. D. Jakes. Bishop Jakes, thank you for all your brotherly, fatherly wisdom and for the inspiring work that you do for God's kingdom. It has propelled my life all of these years. I am so proud of you.

Cheryl Thomas, you are such a consistent blessing to me. Thank you for keeping me organized, copyedited, and encouraged. Thank you for taking the time to comment on each chapter and to provide me with your words of encouragement. At times you were the midwife while I pushed, grunted, and struggled to flesh this book out and onto the pages.

Mrs. Annie Thomas (Cheryl's mom) from New Beginning Church in Gainesville, Florida, I appreciate your prayers so much. Many times I hit a wall and felt empty, and I'd say to

Cheryl, "Please ask your mother and her prayer group to pray." God was faithful to answer your prayers.

Debby Boyd, you are anointed to encourage others and you do that so well. Thank you for reading some of these chapters and providing words to support me through the process. You are a fabulous, uplifting person, and I am blessed to know you.

Tom Winters, you did it again! Thank you for making so many wonderful things happen in my life. I praise God for your wonderful heart and refreshing spirit.

Rolf Zetterson, thank you for the opportunity and the privilege of writing another book for Warner. Warner Faith is doing a great work for God, and I am glad you allowed me to be a part of the mission.

Holly Halverson, it has been delightful working with you. I've enjoyed our conversations and I applaud your editorial skills. Thank you for shaping the pages of this book. God bless you for your kind words to me, your work on this manuscript, and your insight and spirit.

Sister Viola Mays, I thank God for each time you called my office and prayed with me about this book. Thank you for your prophetic words and your words of encouragement. You are a positive lady and a prayer warrior. Thank you for being on my side.

Mother Alice Barksdale, I praise God for you and for the many prayers you prayed over my life and for the completion of this book project. Thank you so much.

Rosa Brown, many times you passed me in the hallway

or on the staircase at work and inquired about the new book. You kept encouraging me, saying that it was going to be great. Little did you know how much those words counted and helped me to press on.

Carla Williams, I appreciate you so much for your interest and belief in this book. Thank you for your prayers and the prophetic words spoken over my life.

Dr. Angeliene Stewart-Pete, you are my friend and my medical doctor too. What a blessing. Thank you for responding to my medical inquiries to help write this book and thank you for helping me to transition back into believing again in the medical profession.

I couldn't close without acknowledging the ladies who allowed me to tell their stories.

Mary Washington, I appreciate your spirit and your testimony. Each time I see you, you are beaming. Thank you for being a beautiful witness in God's kingdom.

Paula White, you are a jewel in God's kingdom and, of course, one of His Trophy Women. Thank you so much for graciously opening your life to my readers. I've found you to be consistently pleasant and a real woman of God. I applaud you, woman of God, for all you are and for everything you do for God's people.

Joni Eareckson Tada, you are an amazing woman and I am proud to share a portion of your outrageously victorious life. I know my readers will be blessed beyond measure to read your testimony.

Annette Hightower Grenz, I am so proud of you and so

happy for you too. God has done so many great miracles in your life. Thank you for letting me share your life with other women. They will be blessed and renewed to learn about your faith in God.

Evangelist Juanita Sapp, I always enjoy our phone calls sharing God's Word. Thank you for allowing me to showcase your outstanding life and give a portion of your testimony. None of us can tell it all. Keep on walking for God and preaching His Word. Your presence alone is a blessing to many, many people.

Isaac, my delightful grandson, I will always remember how you held my hands and prayed a beautiful and special prayer for your Nana and the success of this book.

It's hard to name each and every individual who impacted my life while writing this book, but to all of you, who prayed for me, or who from time to time simply asked, "How's the book coming along?" I thank you.

CONTENTS

FOREWORD

There I sat, on the third step of our extremely modest home, whimpering like a puppy left out in the rain. My eyes were swollen and my heart was breaking. I was maybe seven or eight years old and, yes, I admit it: I had been spanked again. Now, I was by no means the poster child for purity and righteousness. Some even said I was given to mischief, a dark version of Dennis the Menace. But to my sister I was as aristocratic as the Prince of Wales and as innocent as Huckleberry Finn. I lavished in her arms and turned to and fro, basking in her naiveté. I knew she was the most awesome person I would encounter.

I turned up the volume a notch or two on the tears. As I cried uncontrollably in the arms of my sister, I thought I would die of sheer heartbreak; gasping like an asthmatic, I coiled and wrenched violently. Okay, I guess it is safe to admit now: I really wasn't hurt that badly. Perhaps some of the writhing was a way to spark some guilt in my mother. You see, my mother was big on spanking and had never heard of "time out" or allowing your children to process their decisions. Our mother was not easily stricken with guilt. Once she had made her judicious decision, judgment was executed and no chance for parole was mentioned.

My hind end was smarting, but it was my feelings that were bruised beyond recognition. My sister sat with me, comforting me as best she could without alarming my mom, who was an equal opportunity disciplinarian. Jacqueline knew better than to ignite my mother, so she whispered her medicinal words into my ears. She never knew my ears were leaking her loving words into my open heart. My sister, who has an immeasurable ability to comfort and protect those she loves, was there on the spot to rescue and to console me. She kissed away my tears and stroked me while I gasped aloud, peeking around the corner trying to see if my mother might return to repent from her ways and sign a contract to never do such a hideous thing again.

To be sure, my mother never came around the corner nor even seemed remorseful. Therefore the only consolation that remained possible for me was the lifting of a song from the heart of my sister, who loved me even though I had probably done something horrific to get the punishment in the first place. It never mattered to her as she sang me her song to pull me out of the pained environment I was in.

She sang in her contralto voice the old song "Summertime." As I sat there, little did I know that beneath the sting of sweltering skin and emotional shock was a soul who was being comforted by someone whose ability to bring comfort would one day reach around the world.

Isn't it funny how we all need to be loved and encouraged sometimes? I would never tell her, and you'd better not either, that even in my teens and early adulthood, I still drew strength from the lullaby that put my boyhood to bed and caused me to wake up a man. Even fully grown I have, from time to time, wished for those stairs to sit on again and hear her sing those sweet words from "Summertime."

Enough of this nostalgia. Let's fast-forward to this era we are in now. No longer a teenager, Jacqueline is now a woman filled with life's experiences. She has become a mother and grandmother. She is my mother's daughter and my father's joy. She has been married and divorced, healthy and ill, a linguist as well as a prolific writer, but most importantly a thinker. Jacqueline is as full of experiences as a museum. Every shelf is lined with something exquisite archived for connoisseurs who would come to gaze deeply, garnering understanding and storing new perspectives after a visit with her. After years of working for the American Psychological Association, she has seen and worked with the best and brightest minds in the world today. She now writes for our ministry magazines and materials. She has a way of coupling psychology and spirituality with good old-fashioned *Sister Wit*. She often writes what I am thinking.

It is with reluctance that I share her with you. She is a treasure of wisdom and a voice of love. The woman has never lost her ability to nurture the wounded soul and anchor us in her bountiful bosom of intellect and sage-filled insight. As you read the words she has personally penned, know that this is more than a book. It is more melodious than a song. It is the deep elixir that comes from a heart so rich with life that it glimmers in the dark and has an effervescence that transcends a pervasive society. I believe that all who read her work will find it to be a light in a dark place. She reads like a warm blanket and a hot mug of chocolate shared between lovers on a snowcapped mountain.

So my advice to you is snuggle up in a corner. Play some soft music and let my big sissy sing you to sleep with her wit and charm and know that whatever has spanked you, its pain will pass. In fact, its pain has no power to destroy you. It will only transform you while you are safe in the arms of Jacqueline. Ladies and gentlemen, she is more than a *Trophy Woman* to me . . . she is the shine on the brass and the sparkle on the pearl. If she is anything, she is the fine metals that the trophy is made of . . . enjoy her words and learn her spirit until all those you touch are as impacted as I have been by the incomparable wisdom of one woman with a pen in her hands and a song in her heart!

T. D. Jakes

INTRODUCTION

But in a great house there are not only vessels of gold and of silver, but also of wood and of earth; and some to honour, and some to dishonour.

2 TIMOTHY 2:20 (KJV)

When you fall down, get up with something in your hand.

UNKNOWN

All I read about "trophy wives" left a strong imprint on my mind—so strong it finally spawned the book before you: *Trophy Women.* No doubt you are familiar with the expression *trophy wives,* which refers to young, pencil-thin, gorgeous females who marry high-powered, high-profile, older gentlemen. These women are supposed to boost their husbands' egos and professional status.

Some call these women "arm candy." Trophy wives are paraded around at business luncheons and social functions.

Rich husbands spend lots of money on their trophy wives to ensure the envy of their male peers. These women are designed to display their husbands' success. The husbands want to impress, and the wives want to feel secure.

Trophy wives' power is partly their looks and physique, but more important is their age. Their youth is their ticket into the marriage. Recently, many affluent men have added "professional, polished, and accomplished" to their trophy wives' requirements. Still, being very young is mandatory.

In exchange for their youth and their perfect polish, their sugar-daddy husbands shower them with money and gifts. These husbands may set up their wives with their own businesses. The couples' focus is always on wealth and appearance: the rich, aging husbands flaunt their wives as some of their prized, tangible status symbols.

The relationships flow smoothly until the wives begin to age. At that point, the husbands usually trade them in for younger models. Basically, these women are like pieces of jewelry: they are *accessories* to the men. Their trendy lifestyles and their marital job descriptions begin—and end—with their youth and beauty. With these qualities they enhance the lives of their tycoon husbands; without them, these women are no longer useful.

THESE WOMEN ARE LIKE PIECES OF JEWELRY: THEY ARE
ACCESSORIES TO THE MEN.

Now, I am not criticizing age-gap relationships. Not at all. Remember, Boaz was much older than Ruth. Many times, older men successfully marry younger women and vice versa. What I've just described, though, shows what *trophy wives* look like in the world's "kingdom"; what I seek to show in this book is what *Trophy Women* look like in *God's* kingdom.

Trophy Women are a far cry from those I've just portrayed. In fact, the contrast is so stark between trophy wives and the many Trophy Women in God's House that it is fascinating to explore the differences.

Let's begin by looking at the definition of a trophy. *Webster's* says a *trophy* is "something gained or given in . . . conquest."[1] People win trophies for succeeding in battle. Trophy wives—those young ladies who seek out older men for their money and influence—follow a worldly pattern. God's Trophy Women, however, don't follow the trendy lifestyles of this ever-changing world. Trophy Women are indeed the result of battles—life battles they have fought and won—and God has made these women the actual rewards for victory. Trophy Women symbolize accomplishments, while trophy wives symbolize empty pursuits: the wives are bought and traded, not valued.

Yes, God has a different path for His women. While I know how persuasive public opinion can be, and how powerful the influence of the media is, ladies, let us not lose our heavenly directives and our spiritual perspectives on what God desires for us. In this fast-paced world, we are bombarded by opinions and images that constantly redefine who we are as women and what we should aspire to become. How curious that a woman would be rewarded for being young and thin. Why shouldn't she be honored for who she is and what she has endured rather than for what she looks like?

God, who is rich in mercy—God, who is the Author and Finisher of our faith—has a plan for each of His women. By strengthening us to stand through our personal storms, God gives us the opportunity to become cocreators with Him. As cocreators who rebuild the broken bits and pieces of our lives, we have the chance to take the worst and make it the best, to take sorrow and weave gladness, to spin straw into gold. Because we are uniquely tattooed with God's divine imprint, we must walk out our lives with Him, through many "dangers, toils and snares,"[2] and experience His power, His glory, and His majesty.

> WE HAVE THE CHANCE TO TAKE THE WORST AND MAKE IT THE BEST, TO TAKE SORROW AND WEAVE GLADNESS, TO SPIN STRAW INTO GOLD.

You, my sister, are not to be a self-serving woman who seeks careless living but a faithful disciple who takes up her cross and follows Christ. You must not give in to the sorrow of perilous times but come forth triumphant. Through struggle and pain, the Potter shapes and fashions you until you stand like a golden masterpiece: a trophy made fit for His use.

While trophy wives are little more than pleasure seekers who are happy just to shine on their husbands' shelves,

God's Trophy Women are far more valuable than decorations. The Trophy Women I know have withstood many challenges. But the sometimes harsh and fiery winds of life have not broken them; they have survived perilous tests and seasons of distress. They've not always strutted around, finely dressed, or lived lavish lifestyles. But they have become rich in spirit and taken on a value "worth far more than rubies" (Prov. 31:10). They have engaged in battle and won. As a result, these women are trophies in God's curio, treasured possessions of the Most High God.

Do you know any of God's Trophy Women—women of extraordinary substance who possess huge value and distinction? These ladies are God's showpieces! God's Trophy Women represent Him through their living relationships with Him. His Word has been made flesh through their lives. They not only read about healing and provision, but they also have been healed and know firsthand that God is their Provider. These women don't give a testimony of what God can do; these women *are* a testimony of what He can do. These are real women through whom you can see the miracle-working power of God.

God trusts His Trophy Women with trouble. He knows they will come out on top. Ladies, it is an astonishing honor that God—the King of Glory, the Creator of the universe, the Ancient of Days, the One without beginning and with no end—selects you to enter into covenant with Him so that His works may be made manifest in you (John 9:3). You are blessed to have His attention, and it is your plight that has given you front-row seating in His presence. The light and heat generated from being this close to God are reserved only for His Trophies.

Great favor—clout with the King—is released in the life of the woman who has relationship and close association with the Head of all things. Marriages that endure the hard times, the unknown, and the uncertainties of life end with a happy, contented couple smiling into old age. So it is when you walk with God through deep and burning fires. Sharing those difficult experiences with Him, and watching His unfailing rescues and deliveries, births an intimacy that only painful trials create. Your overcoming these fiery ordeals reveals that you are a blessed woman of God, covered with His favor in your life.

In this book, we will look at different Trophy Women in God's House. See in them what God can perform in your life. Look on them to witness His power. God has produced in these women a hands-on knowledge of His might. Trophy Women are eyewitnesses to the deliverance of God. They are women whom life has cast down but who have risen up with fists filled with glory from real encounters with God.

Following each chapter is a poem related to the trophy-making process, some questions for your reflection, and a prayer for your strengthening.

> THESE WOMEN ARE TROPHIES IN GOD'S CURIO,
> TREASURED POSSESSIONS OF THE MOST HIGH GOD.

I wrote *God's Trophy Women* not to celebrate the celebrated—you will recognize maybe two of my examples of Trophy Women—but to applaud and rejoice in the unknown, nameless women who have suffered and yet triumphed and been made into shining examples that you, dear reader, might be encouraged, inspired, and renewed.

So, on the pages of this book are stories of mostly unsung heroines who struggled through their valleys, who would not stop until life handed them their mountaintops. They are women whom trouble and tribulations called away into the presence of the Lord. They are women who have ridden disaster to triumph. These are God's Trophy Women.

—Jacqueline Jakes
JacquelineJakes.com

1

JUST FOR THE TROPHY

Give her the reward she has earned,
And let her works bring her praise.

PROVERBS 31:31

In my den sit numerous awards my daughter, Kelly, won throughout her school years. Some of her trophies are for college math and science competitions; others are for literary accomplishments, Bible fact contests, even beauty pageants. She received her first and smallest trophy for selling the most boxes of oranges to raise money for her Christian school. At six years of age, she understood the significance and special treatment she could get by competing, winning, and having something tangible to show for her efforts.

Isn't it ironic how we can remember the trophies we've won, yet we can't recall last year's Christmas presents? There is remarkable distinction between receiving a gift and winning

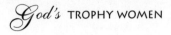

a prize. The addictive and delicious scent of fought-for victory is intoxicating; it brings us pleasure and motivation for years to come. The prize won is more treasured and valued than any handout could ever be.

> THE PRIZE WON IS MORE TREASURED AND VALUED
> THAN ANY HANDOUT COULD EVER BE.

Why? Because everyone loves a winner. And because we value what we have to work for. As a young girl growing up during the fifties in the hills of West Virginia, I said to my mother that I'd love to play an instrument in the local junior high band. After all, I had been playing classical piano for a few years, and musical accomplishments seemed to come naturally to me. But in a state that was less than 4 percent African American, I knew my chances of competing and entering the band were slim—and I said so.

My mother would have none of it. She was a forward-thinking woman who didn't let opposition prevent her from accomplishing whatever goals she set. After all, she was one of fifteen children and a graduate of Tuskegee University!

So off I went to tryouts. I entered and integrated the school band that year and later, in high school, integrated that band as well. When our bands won competitions and we received letters to affix to our school sweaters, I wore my gold and blue, and later orange and black, raised letters on my clothes with pride. I had won a symbol of excellence and had done it against the odds. What seemed an ordinary accomplishment to many other students was a special achievement for me. I had my trophy.

What You *Can* Do

For years I've kept ribbons, trophies, school band awards, and other indicators of accomplishment from my school years. I treasure my tributes from competing and winning. You are probably like me and have an old dresser drawer or a special box in the attic that contains tokens of your successes.

Or maybe you feel you've never accomplished anything noteworthy, or that you haven't become adept at any skill. You'd be amazed at how many things you are capable of but don't take seriously. So many women say to me that they can't write books, but these same women can whip up a dinner that would be applauded at the White House. They may not know how to edit a manuscript, but they can design a hairstyle fashionable and fine enough to wear to the Emmy Awards. I've seen women who could sing until you wanted to dance around the church. So many women don't have confidence in the wonderful things they can do because their gifts don't match those that another sister has.

God has given everyone something. Not all of us have medals and trophies to show for our talents, but nevertheless, each of us has excelled in some area. Whether we have received recognition or not, God knows where our strengths lie. What is important is that we use the talents God has given us and perfect those abilities He has gifted us to possess.

> WHAT IS IMPORTANT IS THAT WE USE THE TALENTS GOD HAS GIVEN US AND PERFECT THOSE ABILITIES HE HAS GIFTED US TO POSSESS.

MASTERING YOUR SKILL FOR A PRIZE

Over the years, I have watched my baby brother, T. D. Jakes, amass innumerable trophies, awards, and tributes for his speaking, writing, and service to people. None were handed to him; he worked hard for and earned every reward he has.

You've watched the Olympics, haven't you? The hours and hours of nonstop competition for the gold are mesmerizing. We hold our breath as we watch each amazing competitor strive to be recognized as the best in the world. We love to see someone win. It gives us hope and makes us proud. It encourages us to go on ourselves and achieve greater things.

The Olympic athletes practiced and competed in smaller contests in hopes of being selected to compete in the Olympic Games. The long, arduous hours of exercising, the consistent drilling and disciplined rehearsals, the strict adherence to special diets conducive to building strong, healthy bodies: all are for just one moment in time, and just for the trophy. Like my brother, these athletes earn each of their prizes through plain hard work. And this is certain: the recipient of the gold, the silver, or the bronze medal finds all of the pain and suffering worthwhile. Those early years of life spent in training, the time devoted to master their skills, prove extremely meritorious to the winners.

I've mentioned that as a young girl, I took classical piano lessons. At eight years old, after I came home from school and completed my homework, I had to practice piano for one hour. While other children ran out to play ball, jump rope, skip, and make up games, I was practicing scales on an old upright piano. I had to memorize sometimes eight- and nine-page piano scores.

You see, I was preparing for recital—the presentation to our parents, teachers, other students, and adults that displayed our progress in the world of music. You'd be shocked at how proficient you can become at a talent if you work at it for one hour each day. Oh my, I'd love to have the time to practice and perform like that today!

The apostle Paul understood races, prizes, and mastery: "Do you not know that in a race all the runners run, but only one gets the prize? Run in such a way as to get the prize. Everyone who competes in the games goes into strict training. They do it to get a crown that will not last; but we do it to get a crown that will last forever" (1 Cor. 9:24–25). And again: "Brothers, I do not consider myself yet to have taken hold of it. But one thing I do: Forgetting what is behind and straining toward what is ahead, I press on toward the goal to win the prize for which God has called me heavenward in Christ Jesus" (Phil. 3:13–14).

GET A CROWN THAT WILL LAST FOREVER.

The apostle Paul wanted to win. He understood his mission, and it was for the prize that he ran, strained, and was persecuted. Later he tells us: "I have fought a good fight, I have finished my course, I have kept the faith: Henceforth there is laid up for me a crown of righteousness, which the Lord, the righteous judge, shall give me at that day" (2 Tim. 4:7–8 KJV).

Trophy Women struggle to win as well. We too desire to receive an award of merit. As Christian women, we know that for our faith in the death, burial, and resurrection of our Lord and Savior Jesus Christ, for our belief in His work of redemption, and for our good works and character, we expect to be rewarded now and in the world to come. Even in this present world, both believers and nonbelievers have confidence in a system of reward. Look at the Grammys.

The Grammy is the music recording industry's most prestigious award. Annually, this ceremony gathers thousands of creative and technical professionals from around the world to witness who will be named Entertainer of the Year. This momentous event is telecast to millions. The awards symbolize contributions, skills, and activities of significance.

Our church group, The Potter's House Choir, has been twice nominated for a Grammy. It is an honor to be nominated and an even greater honor to become a recipient. We were elated when the choir did indeed win the award for its music project, *A Wing and a Prayer.*

My first book, *Sister Wit,* was eventually made into an

audiobook. The audio was nominated for an Audie, an award of excellence. I would love to say I took home the trophy, but I didn't. Still, it felt so good to have been so close to receiving it. Again, it is partly my brush with winning that spurs me on to accomplish other feats.

Not long ago, I sat in the audience with family members, friends, and thousands of other people waiting to see my brother, T. D., receive the President's Award at the NAACP Image Awards Ceremony. Gathered in Hollywood, all of us were dressed in the finest of clothes and jewelry. Excitement filled the air as the name of each nominee was called. Finally, we heard the name of the honoree for the President's Award. We rose to applaud my brother for winning this honor. Needless to say, our row was clapping hands, stomping feet, and shouting words of celebration to show our support. He and his wife, Serita, walked the red carpet, and history recorded a tremendous event.

It is no small thing to win a trophy. It is a symbol of achievement. It is a tangible recognition of success. It is a sign that reveals the difference between victim and victor, losing and winning. It is an outstanding indicator of significance and mastery.

THE DEEP REWARDS OF WINNING

Just imagine it: You are the winner of the highest award an organization gives. You receive a trophy to symbolize and celebrate that you have competed and won. Your satisfaction is great, because you alone know how hard you strove to obtain the prize. You endured brutal training and fierce preparation to win. Winning the award denotes greatness and victory.

> WINNING THE AWARD DENOTES
> GREATNESS AND VICTORY.

This is why, year after year, football players work to build more muscle mass, endure countless practice sessions, continue a restricted diet, and maintain a positive attitude. Imagine the hard work of those competing for the Heisman Trophy. The Heisman is awarded to this nation's outstanding college football player. The work involved is unimaginable. The commitment to stay in the game in spite of sore muscles and aching bodies is tremendous and impressive. Winning takes hard work.

In the movie industry, millions of dollars are spent to produce a first-class work of art and to bring home a trophy: the Oscar. That small golden statue is the final word on who is the best that year. Each nominee hopes to walk away with a visible declaration, a sign, an announcement to the world of his or her talent. To be the recipient of an Oscar is to be marked with the industry's seal of approval.

Whoever receives the small golden statue would never sell it. He wouldn't throw it in the laundry room. He wouldn't set it on the balcony or lay it on the porch. It won't be splashed with gravy in the kitchen window or gather dust in the attic. The person who receives this trophy displays it in a prominent and a safe place for all to see. The trophy has value. The trophy is a message to others proclaiming triumph.

As I write this, I have just hung up from a conversation with a young woman, now graduated from a prestigious university, married, a mother, and gainfully employed. When I told her about the first chapter of my book, she reminded me of her own childhood. She was a second-grader in a single-parent home, living in a substandard house and watching her mother recuperate from a life-changing illness. She began to describe how she felt as a little girl making fires in the fireplace to keep the house warm: her little hands hurling the big logs and huge chunks of coal into the wood-burning stove—a task for someone many years older. But for her, it was an opportunity to help her ailing mother.

The days were dark with sorrow in her tiny home, so she used every opportunity to be cheery and to make her mother laugh. Laughter was priceless to them. Both she and her mother continued their journey through the foreign season, praying, praising, and believing the Word of God.

No one had prepared my friend to live with an ill mother. From day to day, she did not know if ultimately her mother would live or die, but she watched her mother grow closer to God and she grew closer to Him too. Out of the ashes and decay, many, many long years later, she now realizes her salvation, personality, character, and perception had come into existence, had been, in fact, shaped by her experience as a child dealing with adult issues. Today, as a strong Christian woman, she says it was trusting God to keep her mother

alive and to make her little life better that prepared her to successfully embrace her own journey through life. She endured the adversity God called her to face, and she became a Trophy Woman.

So many of us do not regard God's individual pathways for His women. If we are believers in Jesus Christ, all things work together for our good. We have to know that if God allows some struggle, some tragedy, or some imposition in our lives, He must have a greater purpose. Pay attention to what God allows to happen to His children. He is a Master Planner. Nothing escapes His review, His architectural rendering, and His ultimate plan. Ladies, if we are blessed and highly favored, we trust He is in charge at all times and over all things. He really does have the whole world in His hands, and that includes you and me.

MEET A TROPHY WOMAN: JONI EARECKSON TADA

This is really a wonderful place for me to introduce to some and to reacquaint others with a remarkable lady who knows firsthand trouble and testing, yet she continues to overcome every obstacle. I first heard of Joni Eareckson Tada some years ago. I remember seeing some pictures of a young lady in a wheelchair with a brush in her mouth, who created exquisite paintings and pictures. I was amazed. I am still amazed that she was able to do that. You see, Joni is a paraplegic. She is a Trophy Woman in a wheelchair.

Joni broke her neck and suffered the resulting disability

in a diving accident at the tender age of seventeen. For over thirty-five years, she has not walked. But Joni's mind—oh my, what a mind!—has always been powerful. She is an extremely strong believer in the Lord Jesus Christ and has learned to utterly depend on Him.

Joni requires total care for all of her physical needs. Still, I don't know if I would describe Joni as disabled. She bears so many roles and responsibilities. She is an activist for the disabled worldwide. She was instrumental in birthing the Americans with Disabilities Act through her three-and-a-half-year presidential appointment to the National Council on Disability. She is also an author of over thirty books, is a much-sought-after conference speaker, has her own daily radio show, and has created her own organization years ago (www.joni.us). She is a woman with a fierce determination to live her life to the fullest.

When I say *to the fullest,* I don't exaggerate. Are you aware that after Joni became a paraplegic, she married? She has been the wife of Ken Tada since 1982. You could write volumes about this mighty woman, but I wanted to briefly showcase a little of her inspiring life as one of God's Trophy Women.

When I asked Joni about her life, here is what she wrote me:

If living as a quadriplegic for 3½ decades has done anything, it has bankrupted me, leaving me emotionally and physically decimated. But that's not a bad thing. For suffering has served as a sheepdog, forcing

me down the road to Calvary where I might not naturally be inclined to go. Suffering has pushed me into a spiritual corner, causing me to seriously consider the lordship of Christ. Radical dependence on God is a great way to live. It's the 2 Corinthians 1:9 way to live, for ". . . this happened that we might not rely on ourselves but on God." I am not ashamed to say that when I wake up in the morning, I often think, *Lord Jesus, I have no strength for the day, no smile. May I please borrow your smile?* Before I get out of bed, God infuses grace into my heart and implants a bright perspective on the day. Perhaps the really "handicapped" people are those who go at life under their own steam, for "God resists the proud." Oh, the wisdom and grace of God! "Therefore I will boast all the more gladly about my weaknesses, so that Christ's power may rest on me." (2 Corinthians 12:9)

Only a Trophy Woman of God could say that being "emotionally and physically decimated" is "not a bad thing." Trophy Women see the beauty behind the tragedy, the gain behind the loss. Their belief provides the power they need to keep going—and shining!

WORDS FOR THE WEARY

Doubtless some of you are so weary of walking in the midst of a struggle that you cannot begin to think of winning a prize. More than likely, your life doesn't look like a success and you don't feel like trophy material. You are just trying to survive.

I understand completely. But you must ponder the French proverb that says, "No rose without a thorn." Or I might say, "No trophy without a trial."

It is so effortless for someone to lecture others on how to live well, strive for mastery, and run the race of life with dignity. Anyone can give direction when all is well and when he or she is living normal, boring days. But if you are facing a deep struggle, a seemingly endless physical, emotional, or mental war, it becomes increasingly difficult to put up a face against monumental adversities. Sometimes, no amount of prodding seems to help you to keep your eyes on the prize.

I know—life sometimes can feel like a cocoon of misery. When it does, one enters the greatest battle of the soul: the battle to believe. Yes, we love a winner. Yes, we want to win. But often discouragement leans upon us and whispers that things will never change. At times like these, you must wrestle your own soul to force it to believe the Word of the Lord. Believe that life will again say *Yes* to you, that circumstances will once again be favorable to you. At those times we must command our souls to bow to the Word of God. (I will share some of my own battles of the soul in the pages ahead.)

As you continue to read, remember that nothing is too hard for God. You must continually believe that He is able to do exceedingly, abundantly above all that you may ask or think. Belief is the beauty and the power, the secret weapon

of every woman of God. We are charged to believe the impossible. When you are at an all-time low, recognize that your circumstance is a distraction seeking to keep you from your deliverance and your destiny. Trouble sometimes comes to test our faith and to make us strong. Our response is to believe. Quite simply, *believers believe*.

> BELIEF IS THE BEAUTY AND THE POWER, THE SECRET
> WEAPON OF EVERY WOMAN OF GOD.

No matter what you are trying to accomplish in this life, in order to win at anything, you must do the work necessary to achieve your goal. The extreme spiritual workout you may be undergoing is like a physical workout in a gym. The relentless hard work will discourage the average person from doing well; the winner keeps her eyes on the trophy. In God's House, the winner actually becomes a trophy: one of God's Trophy Women.

Night Vision

For at least an eternal moment
Allow me to pause
Selah
From a formerly unscented lifestyle
To feed upon this unexplored territory
And this exhilarating journey
You place before me.

Now I can set aside stored-up pain
And You can burn away unexpressed feelings
And I can enjoy
This metamorphosis
So stunning and so highly flavored it creates
My future, my destiny, and my
Reality.

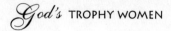

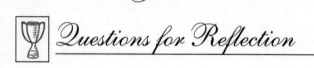

Questions for Reflection

❧ *When have you experienced the "delicious scent of fought-for victory"? What prizes have meant the most to you, and why?*

❧ *Of all the talents you might have, which do you desire most?*

❧ *Of all the talents you have, which do others desire most?*

❧ *Describe one incident in your life when you endured and won. How was this saying true for you: "No trophy without a trial"?*

❧ *What is the "secret weapon" every woman of God possesses? How did you use this tool during your last trial?*

# *Prayer*

Father,

In the name of Jesus, I thank You for Your grace and mercy extended to my sister through the shed blood of Jesus Christ. I praise and thank You for allowing her to experience the richness and the vastness of Your salvation. Because I know that Your redemption includes all of her brokenness and all of her errors, I ask You now to reveal to my sister how completely she is forgiven, loved, and cherished. Bless her to see that You are mindful of her situation and that as she yields her life to You, You will correct her emotional pain. Let her know explicitly that You hold the key to her broken heart: remind her that tough times demand more of Your care and mercies, but they are freely available to her.

Father, bless this woman to become a recipient of Your kindness; let her have a head-on collision with Your mercy, Your gentle, sweet Spirit, and Your healing love. Overshadow her with so much of Your goodness that she is purged of her past and is unable to do anything but acknowledge Your mighty hand changing her life. Let her life be so remarkably changed that others are renewed by this root work You are now beginning in her life.

In Jesus' name, amen.

2

THE WORK OF AN ARTIST

O LORD, thou art our father; we are the clay,
And thou our potter; and we all are the work of thy hand.

ISAIAH 64:8 (KJV)

A trophy is generally made of a substance that had to be developed. When we witness the recipient of an award holding her prize high in the air, everyone cheers. The winner holds an exquisite piece of metal that has gone through many processes to produce the stunning, shining results. We see a work of art. But we have not seen what has taken place to produce the trophy.

We haven't witnessed the many procedures to customize the award of recognition. You and I were not there as the concept for the trophy's design was birthed and danced its way onto the consciousness of an artistic soul. Nor were we present when the craftsman began to sketch and later fashion the masterpiece into a reality. When the trophy is waved high, no one thinks of the hard work of casting, smelting, refining, and forming the trophy. We see only what the trophy represents: triumph.

And so it is with our lives. When we finally "come forth as gold" (Job 23:10 KJV), few have witnessed the process that led to our gleaming outcome. But before any great thing or great person is fashioned, rigorous manipulations and extreme conditions have prevailed.

> BEFORE ANY GREAT PERSON IS FASHIONED,
> RIGOROUS MANIPULATIONS AND EXTREME
> CONDITIONS HAVE PREVAILED.

Look with me at Genesis 2:7: "And the LORD God formed man of the dust of the ground, and breathed into his nostrils the breath of life; and man became a living soul" (KJV). On the sixth day, God created man. His creation with two legs, two arms, two ears, two feet, two hands, two eyes, one head, and millions of nerves and nerve endings, with countless parts to help him function at maximum capacity, was a miracle. God created His brilliant composition to withstand the elements, to think, to move, to learn, to know, to breathe, and to function from an impeccably designed hard drive: the brain, so perfect and profound that man has yet to use it to its full capacity.

God's skillfully constructed man is so remarkable it cannot be duplicated. The Scriptures say that God formed man from the dust of the earth. He gave dimension and structure to Adam's body. But He didn't stop there. The Scriptures say that He continued to create: He breathed into that form and Adam became a conscious being. Eyes wide open, blood flowing, warm body moving, brain thinking and discerning: man became "a living soul."

No trophy manufacturers can put so much work and creativity into their products that they compare to what God put into His fine creation, but there is some similarity in the process. Both God's creation and man's inventions are carefully planned and constructed so that they bring into being a unique and fine specimen, an exceptional final product.

> GOD'S CREATIONS ARE CAREFULLY PLANNED
> SO THAT THEY BRING INTO BEING
> AN EXCEPTIONAL FINAL PRODUCT.

The winner grasps the shiny and lustrous metal with no thought that it has gone through a casting process to make it strong and durable. Metals are liquefied and poured into forms to give shape and pattern. Depending on the particular type of trophy, it might have been etched and engraved before plating for a meticulous finish. Imagine if the trophy were a living soul: what must it feel like to be brought to completion? Imagine being melted down, poured into a mold, sanded, detailed, carved, and then buffed, scrubbed, and rubbed until the artist can see his image in your surface.

Ouch! It hurts to even think about such handling and treatment. But that is what it takes to make a trophy . . . and a Trophy Woman.

So, too, God molds and melts us, then shines us until He can see His image in our surfaces. The process that makes a trophy shiny and durable is just like the process that makes Trophy Women radiant and strong. Women who are blessed and highly favored will exude these qualities.

Is it any wonder people love to possess trophies? Trophies represent time, skill, and value. If you are one of God's Trophy Women, what gives you value?

MEET A TROPHY WOMAN: PAULA WHITE

Paula White began life in a happy, well-to-do family, but at the tender age of five she saw life change. Her father committed suicide, and her life spiraled downward in every arena: emotionally, socially, and financially. To make matters worse, between the ages of six and thirteen, Paula was physically and sexually abused.

Not surprisingly, she became driven to find acceptance, love, and relief from her trauma. Paula did this by immersing herself in school functions and her studies, maintaining a high grade-point average. But while she was busy hiding from life and running from her abuses, God had another plan for her life. When Paula was in college, she met the uncle of a friend. The man took one look at her and said he could see through her carefully guarded mask; he could see pain deep within her soul and suffering in her eyes. He began to minister life to her through the Word of God.

Although Paula had seen many counselors, none of their techniques had been therapeutic. Nothing had pierced her spirit until this encounter.

Amazingly, Paula had driven by churches but had never been introduced to Christ. She had attended funerals but never heard preaching. Consequently, she didn't know anything about the Lord. In fact, to her, "church" was merely another building, one without meaning.

Although it is a terrible thing to hear that in this country someone has never heard the gospel preached, Paula's unawareness was a setup: God used this fresh knowledge of Himself to fill the thirsting within her soul. When her friend's uncle began to open the Bible and share with her medicine for her pain, her eyes were opened.

The man walked her through the Bible, prayed with her, and told her to find a church home. Paula obeyed, and for the next two years of her life she devoted herself to studying the Scriptures. She says the Word of God brought the love that ignited change in her life. Paula says that life is filled with challenges and opportunities, but she believes God wants us to face our adversities equipped to win. She believes God wants us to turn our stumbling blocks into stepping-stones.

Today, Paula White is one of the leading ministers and evangelists of the twenty-first century. She copastors Without Walls International Church in Florida with her

husband, Randy White; hosts an international television program watched by millions; spearheads humanitarian efforts worldwide; and travels the world fulfilling her mission and call to transform lives and win souls. All this from a former "messed-up Mississippi girl." Today, Paula's winning spirit, vitality, and love of God continue to bless multitudes. She is one of God's Trophy Women.

What stands between you and your dream? What happened to you as a young woman that has weighed you down into adulthood? I want you always to remember Paula and her outrageous comebacks—her habitual triumphs throughout life. She manages to walk by faith and not by sight, and we must follow her example in order to advance, succeed, and thrive. She glows with God's love having made her blessed and highly favored.

THE SKILL OF THE ARTIST

The processes we go through create the content of our souls—and it is this content that makes us precious to God. Like Paula, we are all a compilation of our experiences. All of what we take in and encounter shapes our character and our personalities. God allows us, in a climate-controlled environment, to produce the exclusive results that come only from His meticulous planning.

> THE PROCESSES WE GO THROUGH CREATE
> THE CONTENT OF OUR SOULS.

It's the skill of the Artist that makes the difference. When I was a girl, my mother grew all of our vegetables. She also planted flowers in and around our little yard in the dark soil of West Virginia. She could grow almost anything. Her knowledge of when to plant, when to prune, and when to harvest made her garden thrive.

I remember watching her carry water up the street to the vacant lot she had purchased and turned into a garden. As a little girl, I stood nearby while she sprinkled various powders on some of the plants to keep bugs away. I can still see her pinching back the tops of other plants and flowers to force them to bloom and to multiply. On our back porch sat little jars and coffee cans filled with old coffee grounds and crushed eggshells: Momma's homemade concoction to feed her plants and make them flourish. From her creative design and diligent work, we ate supremely healthy and hearty food.

God grows and causes us to bloom through His special concoctions. He soaks into our souls the experiences that will cause us to prosper and thrive. He is tending the garden of our souls, making us rich in character and quality, causing us to be refined and exceptional. Ephesians 2:10 says, "For we are God's workmanship, created in Christ Jesus to do good works, which God prepared in advance for us to do." He provides the seasons of our lives to fashion us into uncommon works of art.

HE IS TENDING THE GARDEN OF OUR SOULS.

Parents as Artists

Have you ever watched the life of a well-raised child? After that child grows up to become an adult, everyone wants either to be a part of his life or to take credit for the work accomplished in his life. On the other hand, I've also watched parents of young teenagers wrestle with their children in exasperation. The parents wonder what happened to the sweet angels they birthed. But many times, those little angels were not consistently guided, carefully monitored, or corrected while young. The parents attempt to administer correction in the teen years, when instead they should have begun to tweak the behavior while their sweet babies wore Pampers.

The guardian over any child has a mammoth responsibility. Not only is she shaping the future of the child, she is also perhaps preparing her own future, which may lay in the decisions of the child she raises. I fear for many parents who do not take the time to fashion trophies out of their own children. It makes me sorrowful when I observe parents who don't recognize the wealth and the preciousness of children. Little ones are empty vessels that you can fill with love, guidance, and every good thing you know about life. Missing the opportunity to prepare them to walk carefully and wisely through this world is reckless.

Parents will get a return on their investment, whether good or bad. If they've treated their children as creatures of great value, their reward will follow them into old age. If their impartation is worthwhile, even their grandchildren will bless their lives. Good parenting has long arms and is effective on many levels. Parents will be blessed multi-dimensionally for their work.

Another way to say it is: whatever is put into a person will come out. Just as whatever special concoction Momma used to feed her plants resulted in numerous blossoms and hoards of wonderful-tasting fruit and vegetables, if we put time and effort into growing our children, we'll see great returns. The more skillful the artist, the more refined her art.

A WORK IN PROGRESS

What we take in and consume changes our physical bodies. As the saying goes, we can dig our graves with our knives and forks, or we can create strong bodies to last us through this earthly journey. When you eat a constant diet of junk food, you clog and destroy the temple of your body; when you eat a balanced diet of fruit, vegetables, and whole foods, you nourish that body and cause it to live and feel well.

It is this same principle God uses to build and restructure our lives. Whatever circumstances God allows to be poured and placed into daily experiences—which may seem grievous and distasteful, like some foods—the results net a magnificent life. Like my mother who fussed and made a ruckus over her garden, God tends to us meticulously, watching over every detail.

He, in fact, is making investments in us that we might

produce an abundant harvest of love, joy, peace, and service to others. Though sometimes His pruning shears are sharp, and His prickly and jagged gardening tools are unrecognizable as instruments for trophy-making, they are unquestionably effective.

It is what is on the inside of us that declares and charts our futures. God allows only the attitudes and the actions that reflect His presence to remain a part of us. Everything else has to be removed. The dross He burns away throughout the process of making us trophies.

> IT IS WHAT IS ON THE INSIDE OF US THAT
> DECLARES AND CHARTS OUR FUTURES.

Webster's defines *dross* as "the scum that forms on the surface of molten metal; waste or foreign matter; impurity; . . . inferior."[1] And Proverbs 25:4 says: "Remove the dross from the silver, and out comes material for the silversmith."

When we are filled with anger, jealousy, and pride, these and other pollutants are what God must burn away through our human experience. As God removes all of the junk, the noxious waste, from our lives, little by little we become vessels of honor that shine like the stars of heaven. God wants His heavenly curio lit up with only the finest display, made up of the highest-quality material: pure gold. But to get the gold, we've got to go through fiery tests and trials to purge our lives of the contamination that make us toxic.

Ouch! Don't you feel like a work in progress?

What Love!

I've said that whoever gets a trophy receives a work of art, a work of genius, a masterpiece made from the finest materials. The divine Artist creates only the best. His Trophy Women wear tags that are gold-foil-embossed: *Made by God*. Do we really expect Him to do anything less than extreme and radical work in our lives?

As He works on and fashions you, it is imperative that you know God loves you. You must be conscious that this almighty power—the Creator of the universe, the King of kings, the One who made all things that exist, and the God beside whom there is none other—loves you and me madly.

If you don't know that He loves you, you won't easily undergo the process of refining, nor will you readily recognize what is happening to you while you endure His trophy-making. You will not see His loving hand working through adversity. You will, in fact, be confused when you watch your life melt down! But if you are intimately acquainted with His love, you will rejoice and give thanks when He begins the casting process to shape you into a vessel of honor.

Because we live in a blemished and unlovely world, in an often loveless society, we find it hard to fathom the love of God for us. So many women entered this world without love. Many were raised by people who refused to love. The culture in which we live is preoccupied with acquiring materials and net worth—to the exclusion of all else. We should indeed enjoy material goods, but we should really relish love, family, and friends.

This generation, for the most part, has its priorities out of order. Many women have married and have not been loved. Others don't bother to consider marriage because they too rarely see examples of happy homes. Repeatedly, a good number of women have focused on survival and meeting the basic needs of others; they have lived most of their lives without experiencing the richness, the reality, and the vastness of God's love freely available to them.

It is not the will of the Father that His love should be unfamiliar. It is His desire that we know the love of God and His many benefits for the women He greatly cherishes. Ladies, God feels passionate concerning you. Do you know it? Can you see the myriad ways you are indeed "blessed and highly favored"?

GOD FEELS PASSIONATE CONCERNING YOU.
DO YOU KNOW IT?

The Scriptures declare that God's love is impenetrable by outside forces: "Nor height, nor depth, nor any other creature, shall be able to separate us from the love of God, which is in Christ Jesus our Lord" (Rom. 8:39 KJV).

What love!

We are in need of the Holy Spirit to show us how to distinguish and to perceive correctly God's love. For the Bible states: "How great is the love the Father has lavished on us, that we should be called children of God! And that is what we are!" (1 John 3:1). Trying to see, sense, and live in the love of God is far-reaching. He loves us intensely. It's enough to send our minds spinning for decades.

God's love should be a familiar and common part of your connection with Him. Because numerous ladies substitute church attendance for His love, a great number of them fail to see the opportunities to have personal, loving communion with the Savior. But it is vital for you, a Trophy-Woman-in-the-making, to fully enjoy your spiritual union with the God who loves you and desires your companionship.

Though others may be unaware of how God the Artist is shaping you, let the love of God transform you into a stunning showpiece for His heavenly display. Allow Him to put His Master's touch in and around your life. Do not be weary. Faint not. Be encouraged and comforted. The work He will perform in you will reinvent your entire life.

In fact, Trophy Woman, He has already started.

The Master's Touch

When it comes to Him
Let Him be the tender
Firelight that glows in the midst
Of your midnight.

Let Him be the fresh and delightful
Spring that spills fountains of calm,
Clean water into the heated, frantic pool
Of your heart.

When it comes to Him
Give Him permission to make
Alterations to unpleasant atmospheres
And still unkind voices.

When it comes to Him
Let Him scatter sunshine on your gloom
With many smiles and much laughter.
Allow Him to
Softly sprinkle the stardust of kindness
At your feet.

And always when it comes to Him
Let Him fascinate you with His authority,
The wonder of His power and the mystery
Of His way.

Let Him touch you and mold you and form
You with His indescribable Light
As He commands your life
With His Word
And even the sound of His silence.

Questions for Reflection

🌾 *When have you felt God's melting and molding as He's shaped you into a Trophy Woman? What circumstances did He use to "buff" your surface?*

🌾 *How does Trophy Woman Paula White inspire you? Have you allowed any setbacks to stop your pursuit of your dreams?*

🌾 *If you could describe the content of your soul, what words would you use? Are the words negative, positive, or both? (Is the content of your soul growing richer or shallower?)*

🌾 *How did you feel when you read that "God feels passionate concerning you"?*

🌾 *If God is designing you to be a "stunning showpiece," how are you coming along?*

Prayer

Father,

In Jesus' name, thank You for Your complete love toward Your daughters. Thank You for loving us wholly and fully. Like warm spring sunshine, let Your love spread softly around our lives. Open all of our senses to recognize You in every event of life. Whether we are weary from the furnace of affliction or just walking methodically through life, break in on us with the reality of Your strong love. Wake us up and comfort us with Your love. Let us see that You come through other people: Your love shines through the smile of a child and the concern of a friend.

Let us see You sending Your love through the trees, through the sound of music, and through the night air. Breathe Your love upon us, and when we slumber, let us sense Your love in our dreams. Every day, touch us gently with Your unchanging love in ways that are real to us and undeniable to our spirits.

Now, Father, refresh us with Your exhilarating love and let it minister the life You so freely give us.

In Jesus' name we pray, amen.

3

LITTLE WOMEN: LITTLE GIRLS WITH BIG-GIRL PROBLEMS

The childhood shows the man, as morning shows the day.

JOHN MILTON

You have more time to be a woman than you have to be a little girl." That was what my momma said to me when I began to want to wear lipstick and pumps and hose.

There I stood in my dingy white ankle socks, badly scuffed black-and-white oxfords, and oversized, handmade dress, listening to the words of my mother, trying to understand and to heed her advice. Secretly, I knew she was wrong. Somewhere inside, I was certain she was keeping me from the delicious good life she, Daddy, and other grown-ups were privy to enjoy. The worst part was that I couldn't

do a thing about it. In our house, Momma was the boss of the kids (my two brothers and me), and even Daddy knew she was a strong woman with whom he should not trifle.

What I didn't know then was the obvious: Momma was right! Today it seems I've been an adult forever. Now my little-girl days seem at least a lifetime away—a memory, a whisper, long gone and melted in time. And although I wouldn't want to go back, something is wonderful and even magical about those yesterdays. The beauty of innocence is nearly intoxicating.

Sweet are the precious little girls dragging blankets and doll babies, perhaps intuitively practicing for a future occupation of marriage and motherhood. I have listened to eight- and nine-year-old girls whisper and giggle, share stories, hug, and talk. You may have walked past a group of twelve-year-old girls and heard the chatter, laughter, and squeals. These young, tender, innocent females don't have a care in the world, and nothing is more important than entertaining themselves with the fun stuff of life.

Ideally, it should be this way into young adulthood. Shouldn't our early days, our first few years, be lived without burdens? Certainly it should be summertime forever for young people. It was Jesus who said, "Let the little children come to me, and do not hinder them, for the kingdom of heaven belongs to such as these" (Mark 10:14). Apparently, there is something so delightful about children that Jesus says they have something of heaven within—something we should emulate.

> THERE IS SOMETHING SO DELIGHTFUL ABOUT
> CHILDREN THAT JESUS SAYS THEY HAVE SOMETHING OF
> HEAVEN WITHIN—SOMETHING WE SHOULD EMULATE.

Yet, with all of the beauty of childhood innocence, playtime ceases early for a select group of children who have been chosen to experience life's rough edges. No one asks our permission to issue trials. Trouble is never timely. Challenges are not convenient. They do not accommodate our age, lifestyle, family, culture, or timetable. Nor do they discriminate.

Consider Helen Keller, a young girl stricken with a malady that left her deaf and blind. Or take a look at Jairius's young daughter, who suffered an illness unto death at the age of twelve (Mark 5). Or again, my friend Joni, who has struggled with health challenges most of her life.

These may seem to be extreme examples of trouble, but my prayer group has had many children's names on its list. Our prayers have gone upward for children who have been hospitalized for weeks at a time, who have been flown by helicopters to special treatment centers. Some have been in comas, on respirators, on life support. Yet we are watching God restore life, health, and strength to most of these children, one by one.

Why should we expect anything different? The fact is, no matter what a person's age, to be "blessed and highly favored" does not suggest ease and success the way television, the latest books, fads, and films depict them. In fact, to be blessed and highly favored signifies difficulty, confusion, and obstacles.

> TO BE BLESSED AND HIGHLY FAVORED SIGNIFIES
> DIFFICULTY, CONFUSION, AND OBSTACLES.

MEET A TROPHY WOMAN: MARY OF NAZARETH

When asked how we are, how many times have we answered, "Blessed and highly favored"? When we say that, we are acknowledging that we are King's kids, privileged, prospering, and fortunate. The Scriptures tell us that Mary, the mother of Jesus, was blessed and highly favored: "And the angel came in unto her, and said, Hail, thou that art highly favoured, the Lord is with thee: blessed art thou among women" (Luke 1:28 KJV). But her life did not reflect the meaning we attach to that phrase today.

God knew He could trust Mary with trouble even at her young age. God began to make a shining example of Mary's life in her childhood. Mary, the woman esteemed and exalted among women, experienced problems and potential ruin on an appalling level.

Although God knew He could trust her, Mary did not know she was trustworthy until adverse circumstances began to test her. I am sure that Mary was amazed at the events taking place in her life: she was a child, a mere child, with child and no husband to boot, living in a time when the least bit of promiscuity was considered gross sin.

Imagine with me that an angel has just told us that we are blessed among women. The first thing we would do is begin to praise and worship God. Then we start planning what kind of cars we will be driving, which neighborhoods we are going to build our mansions in, how many kids we are going to have, and how happy we will be with our wealthy, good-looking husbands. After receiving that kind of heavenly message, we would go on and on with our fantasy.

It would never cross our minds that "blessed and highly favored" could mean we would become pregnant out of wedlock, not know the father of the baby, and marry a man who is suspicious of our moral integrity. To us, "blessed and highly favored" would never imply that we would deliver our baby in a barn or that we would flee with our family from one country to another. Look at the woman of God running for her life:

> And when they were departed, behold, the angel of the Lord appeareth to Joseph in a dream, saying, Arise, and take the young child and his mother, and flee into Egypt, and be thou there until I bring thee word: for Herod will seek the young child to destroy him. When he arose, he took the young child and his mother by night, and departed into Egypt. (Matthew 2:13–14 KJV)

I mean really, ladies, who would call that "blessed and highly favored"? Would you? Would you want to be "blessed" if you knew you had to go through what I have just described? Yet, that is what the Bible describes. If we, like

Mary, are going to be blessed and highly favored, Trophy Women, then we'll have to buckle up, because we are going for the ride of our lives on a journey that gets under way in our youth.

> IF WE, LIKE MARY, ARE GOING TO BE BLESSED AND HIGHLY FAVORED, THEN WE'LL HAVE TO BUCKLE UP, BECAUSE WE ARE GOING FOR THE RIDE OF OUR LIVES.

THE TESTS START EARLY

Once a lady in our church preached a message entitled "It's a Dangerous Thing to Say Yes to the Lord." She reasoned that once you say yes to the Lord, He takes you seriously and won't let you out of your verbal contract. I don't know that it's dangerous to belong to Him; I certainly know it is eventful.

Maybe at a young age you had some life-changing experience that shaped your future and altered your perceptions. It did not have to be a large, conspicuous event; it could have been a small, seemingly ordinary occurrence that took place in your tender life to get your attention, to pick at you, to drive you to desert places where you could abide alone with God.

In this twenty-first century, I don't really think young girls get a good chance at childhood. It seems so many children are born full-grown. It's as if they come here knowing so much, understanding things well beyond their years.

(Remember, Eve had that same problem. She woke up married. Go girl!)

In spite of my momma's words reminding me of how short childhood was, I still experienced some grown-up stuff—but not the kind I wanted. Some of you know what I am talking about. Maybe you were one of those children other students teased and harassed. You were ostracized because you were different. You may have felt singled out, and you were—by God. You were picked out to be picked on. You were chosen by Him to walk a special pathway and journey.

Like Mary, you were highly favored. What you didn't know was that to be highly favored meant you were being prepared for battle, for great trials, and for many sufferings. You were set aside as an example, and the testing started in your childhood.

THE BULLIES' TARGET

When I was a little girl, I ran up and down a wooded path alongside a steep West Virginia hill. It was the quickest way to get to and from school, and it was beautiful. I remember quiet, sunny days, watching buttery sunlight filter through leafy, green trees that hung over the partly shaded pathway. The path led up to a huge rock. I had to climb over the rock, sometimes on my hands and knees, especially if it had snowed the night before. Squirrels, rabbits, and chipmunks ran freely through those woods. I heard blue jays and cardinals singing melodies from the treetops.

This path was a lovely one . . . unless I had received a note from one of the class bullies, who sometimes threatened to hurt me. At that point, a very lovely place became a lonely, frightening one too far from home. When the occasional note was passed and the gang of menacing kids followed me like a pack of wolves, life seemed very intimidating.

For the longest time, even into my adult years, I did not understand why kids always selected one or two children out of the entire school to plunge into fights. I hated those times with all of my heart. I quickly learned that in order to survive, I had to fight back. But for the life of me, I couldn't understand the hatred, the challenge, and the ostracism.

Many decades later, what I have discovered in talking to many women of my age who endured similar circumstances is that we never fit. We were never invited to the parties, never considered popular by those crowds. We were distinctively different. Our tastes, interests, and conversations were different. And our being blessed and highly favored meant we had to suffer even as young women.

Little did I know that my childhood afflictions would prepare me for much more intense challenges. Something I learned about myself early on was that I could step up to the bat; I would show up for battle. As much as I hated childhood squabbles and conflicts, I resisted my enemies by any means necessary. I had no idea I would have to use those same tactics on a spiritual level to escape and survive the real battles of life.

> MY CHILDHOOD AFFLICTIONS WOULD PREPARE ME FOR
> MUCH MORE INTENSE CHALLENGES.

Fighting has no appeal to me, but it is necessary if we are going to be victorious. We've noted that trophies are won through confrontation, through conquest, through tests. So often in church, we talk about the old days of "testimony service." People rose from their pews and told how the Lord had delivered them from an illness or from some financial trouble, or how He had restored a marriage or saved a loved one. All of the testimonies were the results of tests. The persons talking had to walk by faith and not by sight; their faith had been tried and tested through adverse and undesirable circumstances.

WHAT ABOUT YOU?

What did you endure throughout your childhood? Are you the darker-skinned person raised with menacing, fairer-complexioned siblings? Perhaps you are the reverse, the lighter-skinned person surrounded by darker individuals and not appreciated for your difference. Were you raised in a home where a parent had a problem with substance abuse? Was the other parent present? Or were they codependent, leaving you without an ally in an unwelcome circumstance? Were you ostracized for your differences?

You may now appear to be the luckiest woman in the world, but only you and God know what took place in your

early days—those memories that are hidden deep within your soul. Dressed up, hair styled, nails manicured, body toned and smelling like roses: hidden behind the quiet smile, couched beneath the gentle laughter, are painful experiences from childhood. "Blessed and highly favored" for you meant hard times, even as a child.

I've talked with many ladies who shared their difficult growing-up years. Softly, these women whisper their accounts of days long gone.

DIFFICULTY BY DESIGN

Ladies, God designs it so. In our youth, in our early days, God begins His master plan to expose us to opposition. Because He sees the past, present, and future all in one glance, He knows that the end is better than the beginning. No matter what we go through, His intention is for good: "'For I know the plans I have for you,' declares the LORD, 'plans to prosper you and not harm you, plans to give you hope and a future'" (Jer. 29:11).

Notice the strategy God uses to expose us to the difficult nuances of life. Underneath the surface of all the drama and turbulence He allows us enough heartbreak, enough rejection, and enough strife to ensure that we will be victorious. Doesn't sound much like favor and blessing, does it? But I remember hearing a report recently that infants who have to struggle with frequent infections become much stronger to fight off future infections than children who were never exposed to germs and disease. Sometimes the very things that we seek to pray away are the very experiences that will one day keep us alive and well.

> HE ALLOWS US ENOUGH HEARTBREAK, ENOUGH REJECTION, AND ENOUGH STRIFE TO ENSURE THAT WE WILL BE VICTORIOUS.

We learn the same lesson from inoculation. When a person is exposed to a controlled degree of a live virus, his immune system is propelled to arise and fight the invading attack. When the immune system fights, it is strengthened, and when the virus appears again, the immune system is prepared to fight harder, to triumph over an even larger dose of the enemy.

Well, isn't that what happens to children when they are exposed to attacks—attacks of negativity, jealousy, betrayal, abandonment—and social and emotional deprivation? Early life experiences shape every child. Children exposed to God-monitored doses of distress are carefully designed for impending battles and ultimate victories that will never take place in the lives of pampered, coddled, unchallenged children.

Don't think for a moment I am proposing that we create a hard existence for our children or that we neglect our roles as good parents. On the contrary: it is God who sets the stage for His children and brings into their lives the events, people, and circumstances that will work for their ultimate good. As parents, we stand by to cheer and comfort them.

I could not shield my only child, Kelly, the absolute delight of my life, from the onslaught of life. Had I chosen her path, no assaults, no negativity, no unkind words, no nasty looks would ever have come near her precious, sweet, and tender ears, eyes, and existence. But, because God wanted her strong, prepared, and able to withstand the wiles of the enemy, He allowed conflict to come against her. It worked for her good and it made her tougher, more adept, more able to withstand attacks and to conquer that which sought her demise. Had she been born with a silver spoon in her mouth, she would not have been prepared to endure the hardness that later challenged her.

THE SECRET OF THE STRONG

So often people want to know the secret of the strong. It is not an ability that can be taught or given away. To be strong is to be challenged and prepared by an event or series of events that took place at an early age. Survivors are the people who have been fortunate enough to have been consistently nurtured and coached by God in resisting the advances of a hostile environment.

We build our character by enduring hard experiences while avidly following God's day-to-day instructions. God is gracious enough to allow only the precise amount of chaos we can stand to create His masterpieces, and He never relinquishes His control over the details of our lives. When we face the fire, "he will . . . provide a way out so that [we] can stand up under it" (1 Cor. 10:13). Therefore, when negative experiences abound, His children—those who are blessed and highly favored—come forth spiritually, emotionally, and behaviorally sound.

> GOD IS GRACIOUS ENOUGH TO ALLOW ONLY THE
> PRECISE AMOUNT OF CHAOS WE CAN STAND
> TO CREATE HIS MASTERPIECES.

What seemed so unfair to you and me as children was actually a childhood furnace God designed especially for us. He designed it to run us straight into His arms. You probably had an early attraction to God. Was it because of the turbulence in your little life? Did God get your attention at a young age because He knew you would need Him early and much, much later in your life? Perhaps you are like me and have always been delighted about God. You always knew that He was the Creator of the universe and your Savior, and when trouble descended into your frail life, you grew to know Him as Lord.

BOOT CAMP FOR LITTLE WOMEN

Trials have a way of accomplishing many things at one time. One is the fruit of patience. Did you notice how God did not always answer every prayer the way you wanted, when you wanted it, and in the way you expected? In God's boot camp for His little women, He works out patience through our

tribulations. Romans 5:3 states: "We rejoice in our sufferings, because we know that suffering produces perseverance." That's not much consolation to a child, but when God has chosen and enlisted you for great things, when He has declared you "blessed and highly favored," He begins building character early in your life.

God desires to take us no higher than our character can keep us. If His plans are for exaltation, you will experience much turbulence at a tender age. When God trains you, He carefully designs incidents and circumstances and builds on these occurrences until your perception changes, your character strengthens, and your need for Him escalates into a passionate one.

> GOD DESIRES TO TAKE US NO HIGHER THAN
> OUR CHARACTER CAN KEEP US.

Not everyone qualifies for His special impartation. When God made you an example to others, it felt uncomfortable and odd. First Thessalonians 1:6–7 says, "You became imitators of us and of the Lord; in spite of severe suffering, you welcomed the message with the joy given by the Holy Spirit. And so you became a model to all the believers." First Peter 4:14 tells us, "If you are insulted because of the name of Christ, you are blessed, for the Spirit of glory and of God rests on you." God's claim on us makes us stand out. The awkwardness we felt was one only the blessed could experience.

SEE A PATTERN?

If my childhood home still stood, I could mark the spot where my mother first told me about Christ. I will never forget how happy I was to hear such wonderful news. I ran off to a corner of our little home that dangled over the side of a West Virginia hill, held up by a four-by-four, to sit and ponder such delicious information. To think that there was someone greater than Momma and Daddy, that I could talk with Him anytime I wanted, that He could live inside of me, and that He loved me: grandiose thoughts for a five-year-old mind. I was delighted to think that such goodness was possible.

Of course, I had no idea that from my acceptance of Him, He had plans for little girls like me. His plans were tough times, hard days. But He and I would go through them together.

What about you? Can you review your life and see the pattern that started in your younger years? Are you able to go back in time and see that, all along, God was setting you up for something big, something grand, something powerful? Of course, you had to go through the process, stand the test, and learn the truth of 2 Timothy 2:12: "If we suffer, we shall also reign with him" (KJV). But there will surely be many days, months, years, and decades before we actually reign with Him—all things according to His schedule, His time.

ALL ALONG, GOD WAS SETTING YOU UP FOR
SOMETHING BIG, SOMETHING GRAND,
SOMETHING POWERFUL.

I would love for parents to pay close attention to their little ones who suffer trials at an early age. Usually afflictions early in life are signs that they are chosen by God. Many times, when the enemy is allowed to trouble our little ones, those difficulties signal that our children have great destinies. Again, God starts early with His strategic and masterful plan.

EVERYTHING WORTHWHILE TAKES TIME

Walking with God is a process. Nothing He has ever created or formed takes shape overnight. It takes many hours, even days and years, to accomplish great things. For example, Creation. Many debate about whether God took seven twenty-four-hour days to complete the heavens and the earth. Some say that the "day" mentioned in the book of Genesis—"And God called the light Day, and the darkness he called Night. And the evening and the morning were the first day" (Genesis 1:5 KJV)—represents a period of time greater than twenty-four hours. Others disagree.

I am not a theologian, and I won't speculate on which is correct. What I will say is that God did an incredible job, and He took His time breaking down Creation into segments, slicing eternity into time. He gave His undivided attention to detail, to color, to timing, to sound, to textures, to smell, all to provide us a beautiful place to house us until our deaths or until He returns to take us with Him into heavenly chambers.

If God spent the time to create with precision, detail, and perfect synchronization every aspect of this planet Earth, would He not take the time to create the precise circumstances that produce, in your life and mine, the outcome He desires to see in us?

KNOW THAT PAIN HAS GREAT RESULTS

In the privacy of your own heart, maybe you knew as a child that God was making something great out of you. Like the precious metals that come forth from the slag after it's retrieved from an intensely burning furnace, you were being tried in the fire. You were being proven. The tests were big ones, and they knocked you to your knees: a perfect position to pray.

> THE TESTS WERE BIG ONES, AND THEY KNOCKED YOU TO YOUR KNEES: A PERFECT POSITION TO PRAY.

Prayer changes things. Trouble and trials caused you to assume a posture of prayer, and this posture became your lifetime stance.

You probably began to pray long, fervent prayers as well as sixty-second prayers. Did you ever whisper a prayer to God and have Him answer you? Did you ever think a prayer to God and found that He answered that one too? It was almost astonishing to hear from heaven, whether you made a minuscule or a larger-than-life prayer request. To openly see the results changed you forever.

Whatever you are going through at this moment in your life, if you belong to God, rejoice! Rejoice because He is in control. Rejoice because He has prepared you for this trial. You are ready to face it, no matter what it takes. Rejoice if things are well. And, if times are grievous and challenging, rejoice. He has allowed them, but He made you ready first.

You see, He saw you as a Trophy Woman before you even knew Him. Trophy Girls, those "blessed and highly favored" from youth, are on their way to becoming Trophy Women!

Baby's Breath

Scared silent. To the bone.
I shrink inside my tiny child soul
And learn with perfection
The art of becoming
Invisible.

Rather than flower with radiance,
Wisely, I shrivel and seek shelter in
Darkened corners
Underneath oceans of absence
Poisonous static sound waves.
I can hear them fight — there are
Monsters in my house.
And when they again finish
Another round of decaying drama,
I am left
Critical, but stable,
Bruised and blinded
A survivor
A simmering miracle
Groping to find
The
Light.

And when I touched the Light
I was strengthened, yes, encouraged
Made whole, complete
Illuminating—a beacon oozing
Brightness from my soul
Like Sunshine on a nighttime backdrop
Cascading radiance.
Aglow!

Questions for Reflection

- *Did you suffer in your childhood? Can you see how facing those troubles prepared you to face other challenges later in your life? How?*

- *Does it surprise you to learn that being blessed and highly favored connotes difficulty, confusion, and obstacles? Could you have accepted the angel's news as Jesus' mother, Mary, did?*

- *Can you see signs in your life of God's favor and blessing? Have you ever misinterpreted some difficult times as being signs of God's displeasure when they were really the opposite? When?*

- *What is the "secret of the strong"?*

- *Is one of your children experiencing serious challenges at a young age? How can you encourage him or her?*

Prayer

Father,

We thank You and bless You for the children of this world. Lord, we humbly bow our heads to You and exalt Your name for giving us the gift of precious children. Thank You, Lord, for counting us worthy to watch over Your special treasures.

Let each woman reading who was raised in a hostile environment—or who has contemplated the mysteries of her own unattended childhood—recognize how special and precious she is in Your eyes. Bless her to see Your hand in every area of her life, to this present day. And Lord, open the eyes of her understanding as to why she had to go through what she went through. Let her know You were in all of her circumstances. Make plain Your plan in her life. May she have a good understanding that all of her life is part of Your plan, and that nothing that ever happened to her was a mistake.

Kiss the children, Father, in their sore places. Let Your light flood their souls and make all things beautiful in their lives—and in the lives of the grown children of this world.

Thank You, Lord, for Your continual healing care.

In Jesus' name, amen.

4

THE MAKING OF A TROPHY

To be knocked to your knees gives you the strength to stand.

Whenever trying times visited my childhood home, I remember my mother saying, "Trouble keeps you at the feet of Jesus." I mentioned some of my childhood struggles in the last chapter. I would soon learn and remember my momma's words as I went through my own personal conflicts.

Today we live in a society, an age, and a generation that strives to experience the good life: a life of perfection. And what is wrong with that? Nothing. But there are so many paths to the pleasant life, and much of what happens along the way to a seemingly happy ending is a lot of toil, struggle, and pain.

Not many people want to talk about the process. We are rightly told to keep our eye on the prize, the destination. But the problem with focusing on only the outcome is that you will be unprepared for the steps the Lord has ordered in your life. Confusion will set in, leaving you overwhelmed and depressed.

Because we don't discuss the nitty-gritty, day-to-day events that happen in the life of a believer, we become disillusioned with the road to greatness. We want a flawless fantasy life filled with perfection and order. But life is not always like that. We soon discover that we are not participants in a reality show. No one is going to come and fix our broken-down homes. No one is going to give us a total-body makeover so we look like beauty queens. If those are things we're expecting, our lives become wearisome and disappointing.

Why are our lives not better? we wonder. Why aren't we happier? Why do we have to go through desert places? We don't understand why afflictions rise. But the Scriptures clearly tell us that God will not leave us in turmoil: "Many are the afflictions of the righteous; but the Lord delivereth him out of them all" (Ps. 34:19 KJV). We *will* triumph.

Most people don't even look life full in the face until an emergency occurs and they are forced to respond to some devastating circumstance. But you and I know that the vicissitudes of the times in which we live require us to be prepared and as proactive as possible to survive.

GET READY

To be forewarned is to be forearmed. But even though we've heard the many statistics of divorce, single parents, and disease, calamities still thrust themselves onto the pages of our lives and catch us by surprise.

Too many of us have found ourselves lying by the roadside, robbed and wounded, like the Syrophoenician who was helped by the good Samaritan. We all know about the times in life where no matter how prepared, how armed and dangerous we are, unseen forces ambush us, and we are left to humbly await a word of encouragement, a stranger's aid, anything or anyone to help us on our way.

> MANY OF US HAVE FOUND OURSELVES LYING BY THE ROADSIDE, ROBBED AND WOUNDED.

More specifically, there is the woman who has found her unsuspecting self in surgery, rearranged, repaired, but remorseful. Or look at the poor souls who did not see their divorces coming—the women who did everything to keep their marriages going but found that staying married takes two people, in agreement. What do you do when you feel ravished, raped, and victimized by life?

STAND UP TO LIFE

You do everything. You do nothing. You stand still. You march on. You shout. You remain silent. You pray and praise.

You cry and believe. You doubt. You forgive. You go on.

These are a few of the things I personally did to survive a craniotomy—an eight-hour-brain surgery—as well as marital failure, single parenting, divorce, living in an old, decaying house that should have been condemned, and feeding my daughter and myself from lunch-portion-sized meals.

My older brother, Ernest, jokes with me to this day about my asking him to dinner with my daughter and me. He remembers being aghast when he saw on the table in a dish one chicken breast, a wing, and a couple of potatoes. We laugh today. But I was so familiar with having little and watching God make ends meet for me, it didn't occur to me that it really wasn't enough food to share with a 225-pound, six-foot-plus man.

My financial struggles might have been less overwhelming had I not been ill for years. I was trying to stand up to life. I went to work, volunteered at church, and raised my daughter. In the midst of all the challenges, I read my daughter stories every night and pulled my weakened body up thirteen stairs to tuck her into bed and say prayers each evening. Somehow I provided her lunch money from little support, then no support, and then excuses and silence.

I WAS TRYING TO STAND UP TO LIFE.

While I paid fees for school bands, piano lessons, and flag corps at my daughter's private Christian school, I was sick, putting buckets under leaky roofs with my face frozen from temporary and partial paralysis, my mind numbed from illness and difficulty. I could go on, but I think you get the picture. Yet I gave God the entire honor and the glory, because I was so glad things were as good as they were. I knew that if God had not been with me, I never would have made it through such excruciating times. I was blessed.

Without shame and self-pity, I admit that I am a sufferer— and I am also a survivor. Sister, I am a Trophy Woman!

THE STORM *IS* PASSING OVER

As we spend time in the Scriptures, you and I begin to understand that tough times are not foreign; they are part of our journey. You and I can take solace in the Word of God, knowing that although the storms come, time, wisdom, and observation help us recognize the difference between a temporary trial and a permanent situation. No storm lasts forever.

You might be undergoing one of the worst trials of your life. I understand. There are seasons of the soul. Momma often said when the good times come, pretend that you can put them into a little jar. When tribulations arrive, open the jar and revisit the season when life was sweeter and brighter, and know that this too shall pass. Nothing is impossible when you are hopeful.

NOTHING IS IMPOSSIBLE WHEN YOU ARE HOPEFUL.

When you are in the midst of discouragement and difficulty, it is hard to imagine that things will ever be different.
While you are struggling through that divorce, and enduring the waiting period of medical testing to see what the
knot is on your hand, searching for a job, trying to continue
your education, and raising that child alone, you can hardly
fathom that life will be good again. But I challenge you to
look to your future.

If only you knew that God is crafting your life through
circumstance, through human experience and struggle. If
only you knew that help is just around the corner, that dark
days are passing, and that your tomorrow is bright and
gleaming—you would lift your head high and put a pep in
your step and a smile on your face. You would see that bright
future on the horizon and slice the darkness with the hope
of the light of the gospel of Jesus Christ.

Search the Word of God to locate the promises that per-
tain to you—the ones that give you an anchor for your soul. I
know you are doubtful that life holds something exquisite and
wonderful for you, but it does. Your discouragement is temporary, and sorrow will begin to fade. God is turning your trouble into treasure, and He is turning you into a trophy. He has
marvelous things in His storehouse just for you.

ENDURE THE FIRE

The strength and elegance of a Trophy Woman lie not in
her outer beauty but in her ability to be pressed down, and

yet like leavening in dough, she rises again and again and again.

Each day that I rise, I become more confident in Him. I have found that after a while, it becomes insulting to God to doubt His hand of deliverance. After He has brought us through so many struggles, we must become convinced of His ability to consistently deliver us and set us free from whatever ensnares or restrains.

This kind of confidence comes only through our day-to-day walk and communion with God. It is in our prayer time, which never ceases, that we see His will and His way for us. It is through conversing with God and listening for His answer that we are consoled. As we talk with the Master and wait for and witness His deliverance over and over again, we begin to know that being brought to a low estate is not a final destination; it is only part of the journey. Everything God calls us to endure is designed to make our lives brush His strength, His capabilities, His mighty favor, and His love toward you and me.

> BEING BROUGHT TO A LOW ESTATE IS NOT A FINAL
> DESTINATION; IT IS ONLY PART OF THE JOURNEY.

What we know about God causes us to flourish. Once you have shared experiences with the Savior, where you and He have walked through darkness together, you have privileged information recorded in the fiber of your soul. This information reminds you that He is Lord, that Jesus is the same yes-

terday, today, and forever. You know the difference between
knowing about Him and knowing Him, because you have traveled through turbulent times together. You bear the exquisite
beauty of a woman who is blessed and highly favored.

IT TAKES TALKING

You can't be in a successful relationship without speaking to
one another. All relationships are built and bettered
through conversation. In your relationship with God, conversation takes the form of prayer. Not the kind of prayer
that is loud and strenuous—you can do that for only so
long—but the kind of prayer where your mind, heart, and
ear are always turned toward God. The kind of prayer where
"nobody" is present, but you speak out loud because you are
aware of His nearness. The kind of prayer that whispers,
"Thank You, Jesus," and "Lord, I'm grateful," all the day long.

If you are challenged with some kind of trouble, look
over your shoulder. Look back to see the many, many acts of
kindness, the many instances of deliverance, and the countless kinds of rescue He has wrought for you. And remember,
if He did that, He will do this for you too.

> LOOK BACK TO SEE THE COUNTLESS KINDS
> OF RESCUE HE HAS WROUGHT FOR YOU.

So often, we want to ask God if our labor and our living
are in vain. We want to know if there is a method to the

madness. We want to know if there is any purpose to the tough times. We want to be assured that, somehow, whatever we are struggling with and stumbling through means something significant.

I know that it does. There is a wonderful Jewish proverb that you might commit to memory. It says, "He that can't endure the bad will not live to see the good."

MEET A TROPHY WOMAN: ANNETTE HIGHTOWER GRENZ

I recently received a letter from a lady I've known for over twenty years. I met her when I was a young woman diagnosed with a brain tumor. It was a dark and frightening time in my life. Annette was the registered nurse who stopped and prayed with me when she saw me waiting to take the many tests that ultimately led to an eight-hour craniotomy. She was the lady God used to anesthetize me for the surgery. I appreciated her kind spirit and stayed in touch with her throughout the years.

Annette herself faced multiple myeloma, a rare form of bone cancer, in 1996. It recurred in 2002. In 2005, she learned the cancer was widespread and more difficult to treat than it had been before; this time her disease required immediate high-dose chemotherapy followed by a stem-cell transplant. The aggressive treatment did not cause a full remission, so at the time she wrote to me, Annette was preparing for another stem-cell transplant, which would cause serious side effects.

She wrote, "I am scheduled to return [to the hospital]

somewhere around the middle of January. I still have to pray about it. I do not like being that sick. The Word says, 'By His stripes, I am healed.' Amen."

Despite all she had endured and what was to come, Annette wrote, "We are sure blessed. My prayer is that you will take the time to be thankful no matter what situation you may be facing. Life itself is a precious gift from God, 'for it is He who gives life and breath to all.'" And she declared, "The good news is that God is faithful."

When I read her letter, I marveled at how God accomplishes so many things through our bad times. When you walk with God, nothing is wasted. Nothing we go through as women of God is useless. Trophy Women always have—and always are—something to show for their troubles.

PUMP UP THE VOLUME

Annette's resilience and persistence remind me of the Shunammite woman:

> One day Elisha went to Shunnem. And a well-to-do woman was there, who urged him to stay for a meal. So whenever he came by, he stopped there to eat. She said to her husband, "I know that this man who often comes our way is a holy man of God. Let's make a small room on the roof and put in it a bed and a table, a chair and a lamp for him. Then he can stay there whenever he comes to us." (2 Kings 4:8–10)

You know her story. She is the woman who befriended the man of God, Elisha. Her kindness was so impressive that Elisha asked what he could do for her. It was Gehazi, Elisha's servant, who noted that the Shunammite woman had no son. Elisha prophesied that by the next year she would be a mother. She asked the prophet not to deceive her, but she did indeed find herself with a son at the appointed time.

Later when her child grew older, he died. The Shunammite woman saddled a donkey and rode furiously to find Elisha. This woman refused to accept death. She refused to leave Elisha until he accompanied her home to raise her son from the dead. Of course, Elisha fulfilled her request, lying on top of the boy until life flowed back into his body. When her son was restored, she picked him up and went on her way.

There are times in life when you have to refuse what you see with your eyes and hear with your ears. Yes, you heard the diagnosis the doctor just gave you. Yes, you realize that you have been selected to choose an early retirement, and yes, you heard clearly the bad report the counselor gave you about your child. But you heard louder what God was saying in your heart.

> THERE ARE TIMES IN LIFE WHEN YOU HAVE TO REFUSE WHAT YOU SEE WITH YOUR EYES AND HEAR WITH YOUR EARS.

What must be done when trouble blares its monstrous noise at us? Pump up the volume! Here's what I mean. Have you ever pulled up to a stoplight with your windows down and heard a loud and obtrusive conversation that disturbed you, coming from the adjacent car? The language might have been offensive; an ugly fight might have been brewing. Whatever the situation, you found yourself trying to create a way of escape from a distasteful environment.

You probably did the same thing I have done. Discreetly, you closed your window and turned up the volume on the car stereo to drown out the unpleasant bickering.

Sometimes the threats of life pull up alongside of you and attempt to divert your attention to a vile and vulgar atmosphere. When you hear the sound of the hoofbeats of Pharaoh's army chasing you, listen for another sound. Quickly remember and rehearse good words and prophecies spoken over your life. Remember the sermon you know God sent especially for you; mentally recite the Scriptures that hold promises contrary to the disharmony that vies for your attention.

Be alert for your coming victory. First Kings 18 tells us that a drought fell upon Israel for three years. When God was ready to reveal His power by ending the drought, Elijah said he heard "a sound of abundance of rain" (v. 41 KJV). Like Elijah, listen for that sweet sound of deliverance on its way to you.

Ladies, when you realize you are in a place of testing, you must begin to utilize many instruments of survival. God is stretching you. Going to the gym is a wonderful activity, but the exercise that will benefit you even more is not found in sweating, groaning, and struggling to walk, run, and pump iron. The kind of exercise I am talking about will not give you a fierce figure. God's kind of exercise involves working the muscles of your faith by believing when you don't want to; building your stamina by enduring each test to the end; and staying spiritually fit through daily effort. The kind of exercise God wants to see in His women gives you tight, firm, bulging, profound faith and unshakeable confidence in His faithfulness. It gives you, a Trophy Woman, a shine like no other.

Don't forget: pump up the volume.

REQUESTS FOR THE KING

I mentioned in the last chapter that sometimes we just think our prayers, and God answers them. Answers to prayer from a microscopic conversation with God show us that He feels our feelings, and that should strengthen our faith. As surely as God is answering whatever prayer we raise, those trials that have brought our souls to their knees have His attention too. God is listening to you. You have an audience with the King, and He knows all about everything that pertains to you. It is such a comforting thought.

If you are a praying lady, I know you have experienced the wonder that comes from answered prayer. A special air enthrones those times when a whispered prayer is uttered

and you are certain no one, absolutely no one, knew your heart's desire but God. Miraculously, the very thing you requested came to pass.

I have had numerous occasions like that. I remember praying once for something so ridiculous that I didn't have the nerve to tell anyone I would make such a request. It was all the sweeter when a nice little car was parked in front of my door and the keys and title were handed to me. No one can convince me that God doesn't answer prayer. It was one of the many times I went into my secret place, contacted my God, and was rewarded openly.

> NO ONE CAN CONVINCE ME THAT
> GOD DOESN'T ANSWER PRAYER.

PRAYER HELPS TROPHIES SHINE

I want you to reconsider the idea that the boisterous prayers are the only ones answered. I learned this lesson on my bed of affliction. For me, recovering from brain surgery was a decade-long experience. Not only did I face an extended physical recovery due to the severity of my illness, and side effects such as memory loss and temporary facial paralysis, I faced emotional attacks as well—the depression that followed was staggering.

I grieved the loss of my health. I was twenty-nine years old, maritally separated, raising a child alone. It was a frightening place to be. I had such alarming physical symptoms: I experienced convulsions and panic attacks. My child's six-year-old voice sounded odd to my ears: chaotic, broken, like static. My body was weak, and I could accomplish only one small task at a time—something quite unusual for me. My eyes wore a dead stare, my blood pressure rose dramatically again and again, and I suffered from sleep apnea.

On several occasions, I distinctly remember lying on my bed, trying to sleep but instead drifting into an altered state, a place where I was mentally awake but unable to move. Each time I found myself in this condition, I was terrified. I could hear the clock ticking, I could hear the wind blowing the curtain against the windowpane, but I could not get out of bed. My little daughter lay sleeping next to me.

I had no idea what was happening to me. I prayed fervently, "Dear God, don't let my baby wake to find me in this condition. Dear Jesus, please help me to move. My God, please, please help me! Give me back the activity of my limbs." I waited and later was able to get up and walk around. In those frightening moments when I couldn't move a muscle in my body, I *could* talk to God. He heard me. (I learned later that this condition was actually unrelated to my brain surgery, but another illness altogether!)

During the day, I lay on my sofa for months. Sadly, I spent most of my time dragging around the house, praying, "God, I can't wait till this is over."

Unbeknownst to me, those were really words of faith. I refused to let go of Jesus. I refused to give up my faith in

God. I continued to read the Scriptures and pray. I attended church services and made a covenant not to utter complaints and chatter about the strange physical and emotional sensations I was experiencing. I was a fool for Christ, and I did what believers do: I believed. I believed God to heal me when I felt like giving up and dying. God wanted my full attention. He got it.

I got busy doing spiritual warfare to ward off despair. I prayed away physical symptoms in Jesus' name. I was led to use Scriptures to withstand the attacks of the enemy. I became a woman armed with the Word of God, dangerous because of my faith. I had to be "foolish" enough and trusting enough to quote a Scripture until it ran like olive oil over my soul, calming me, dispelling anything that sought to destroy me. Each day that something went right or that I was the least bit better, I praised God. I was blessed to know God and have Him with me in the midst of my struggle. I don't know how people manage without the Lord. If He had not been on my side, I would have been swallowed up in horror.

If God had told me I had the faith to come through this kind of battle, I would have doubted Him. But because He walked me through it and taught me how to pray and touch heaven, I am a violent *believer*. God showed me in my midnights how to accept the light through prayer, faith, and patiently waiting on His presence in silence.

You can talk to God in sign language. He hears you. You can send a telepathic message to God. He hears that too. You can e-mail God from your computer. The point is: *communicate with Him*. He is waiting to hear from you.

God is awesome and He is real! God is allowing you to know His ways, to know Him. He is making certain you are a woman of excellence who knows her God and knows how to contact Him. He is revealing you as one of His blessed and highly favored women. He is making sure you shine.

Trophy Women recognize through the Word of God that they have entered a season of testing. You know when you are on God's workbench, and like any well-made trophy, you submit to the complete process that will cause you to come forth as pure gold. All the melting, pounding, and chiseling are forming an exquisite masterpiece.

When life is difficult and you are under the enemy's attack, prayer changes you or the situation. It gives you the stamina to stand. It gives your surface a sheen. If God has allowed a season of testing, then through prayer He will give you the strength and the grace to get through it. It is exciting to know that regardless of what you face, if God is on your side, *all is well* in your world.

GET SOMETHING OUT OF THE SITUATION

No matter where you are in life, get something out of it. Remember: "When you fall down, don't get up empty-handed."

I listened to a young woman on television some time ago talk about what it is like to live without one leg. This woman never bemoaned her lot in life. From childhood, she had

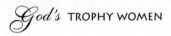

had challenges. She talked about how she experienced pain in a leg that she no longer possessed. Rather than focus on her suffering, she used the pain to help herself use her prosthesis correctly. She explained that she maneuvered her prosthesis to wherever she felt her real leg would have moved to assuage the pain. The pain actually became a compass for her to follow, enabling her to walk again.

When life comes down on you like a hammer, use whatever comes against you as leverage to get up. Use whatever assails you as a weapon to succeed. Get something out of your hard places.

From my ten-year recovery from brain surgery, I gained a hold on God I have yet to lose. I need Him in ways others do not. I understand that life is frail. I cannot afford to distance myself from Him.

God has anointed you for your problem, and He knows you are able to withstand and to stand. Don't lose heart. Remember my friend Annette, who at our last contact has received a clean bill of health and is cancer-free. God is making a prize of His women. Remember to *lighten up* and to keep your mind on Him. Trust God.

WHAT DID I JUST SAY?

I know you cannot believe that I am telling you to lighten up. With all the challenges you face, surely I must be joking. I'm not. Allow me to share with you what I heard God whisper in my ear many years ago. After my brain surgery, the loss of health, loss of job, loss of marriage, and loss of any semblance of financial stability—when all of that dust had settled, I heard these words: "Did you ever have to worry?"

My first response was about to be, "Do you know what I've been through? How in the world could I not worry?" I was shocked at the idea. But then I had a quiet knowing. I began to reflect, and I remembered how God had stayed with me, comforted me, and delivered me out of each terror. I had come to know God as my Deliverer, my Savior, my Bridge over troubled water. I was eyewitness to His provision, faithfulness, and goodness. Joy came in the morning, but oh how long the night. God had gotten me through a night season that lasted a decade.

> JOY CAME IN THE MORNING,
> BUT OH HOW LONG THE NIGHT.

If I had known throughout my ordeals what I ultimately learned firsthand—that God is a very present help in the time of trouble and a sure Deliverer—I would have stressed less. I would have lightened up! I would have looked more toward my morning and not gotten so bogged down in my night.

What are you going through that looks as if it will never end? Approach that problem from the other side of the battlefield. Look at your situation as if it is over. That perspective will empower you to become lighthearted, hopeful, and encouraged. I know it seems impossible, but go ahead: try

directing your thoughts toward your bright future, and see if you don't perk up. What have you got to lose? You will be annoyed with yourself when you come out safely on the other side and realize you increased the weight and darkness of your trial with worry.

Do not be afraid to let go of anxiety and negativity. They are bad habits. I know it seems irresponsible to make merry, but fill your spirit with sunshine. A merry heart *is* like medicine. It does wonders for your soul.

It is so critical that we cast our cares and keep our minds on the Lord. Most of us know how to rehearse destructive images, sayings, and conversations day after day. But we know that negative, repetitious behavior works as a dead bolt to keep us locked into the same state of mind.

If we are going to change our outer circumstances, we must truly seek to change our minds. Keeping our focus on Christ because we trust in Him causes us to see our lives differently. It frees us to view the world from a different room. Our perceptions color our experience, and what we tell ourselves determines how we live, feel, and operate in this world.

> WHAT WE TELL OURSELVES DETERMINES HOW WE LIVE,
> FEEL, AND OPERATE IN THIS WORLD.

When you choose to keep your mind stayed on the Lord, your only option is peace. It is when we ponder His goodness, dwell on His ways, and caress His mercies; when we immerse our minds, our souls, and our hearts into a higher realm, that our day-to-day living becomes an exciting discovery. Our once-troubled souls become quiet and calm places as we delve into the less-traveled world of contentment, love, and joy. Remember, He is our peace.

Keep your mind fixed solidly on Him, habitually making a mental ascent onto the highway of heavenly thoughts that are infinitely good, true, lovely, and pure. Then, no matter how intense the trophy-making process, you can reside in the restful presence of the Prince of Peace.

Gold Dust

Captivated by the intense flames
I stood speechless and witnessed
The sprinkling and scattering of
The remains
Of a life sacrificed.
I solemnly marveled at the fragments
Of the Refiner's Fire: the shining pieces,
The magnetic pieces
That
Glitter like sprinkling sunshine.

Embracing the earth were the
Specks and flecks of what's been left behind,
From the altar of fire
From the execution, the public
Disgrace, the horrid humiliation,
I observed a life that had been
Ground to a shining powder
Only to expose what really matters.
Dazzled by the brilliant display
It's as if I could hear someone
Victoriously say,
"You can never touch this again!"

Questions for Reflection

- *Describe a time when you felt "ravished, raped, and victimized by life." How did you decide to "stand up to life" at that point? Were you successful?*

- *Do you believe that God "has marvelous things in His storehouse just for you"? What do you hope He has stored up for you?*

- *If you are in a place of testing today, how can you "pump up the volume"?*

- *If you treat prayer like having "an audience with the King," how will your prayers change?*

- *Does Jacqueline's advice to "lighten up" sound possible for you? How can you try to lighten up even today?*

 *Prayer*

Lord,

I thank You for my sister who has undergone so many intense trials. Father, bless her to know You as her strength. Bless her to experience You as strong medicine for all of her trials. She may not yet understand that You have built her to pass each test and trial, so right now I ask You to open her eyes to see You working in her situation, making her stronger through each and every thing she has encountered.

Let her look over the days of her life to see her long résumé with You. Encourage her to see that if You brought her through all of the past small and large struggles, the thing she faces today is not too hard for You. Remind her, God, that you are God of all things and that you are her God. Cause her to remember Your promises: You are a very present help in the time of trouble, and for her to have You on her side is to have more than enough strength to face the world against her. Calm her, God, with Your might and strengthen her with Your presence.

Let her rest in You. Let this woman drink refreshing, inspiring, life-giving words into her soul, even in the face of her enemies and in the midst of her situation. Whisper repeatedly into her heart that you will always cause her to triumph. Let her be strengthened by Your faithfulness and Your Word and by the fact that You will bring her to an expected end—a glorious outcome.

In Jesus' name, amen.

5

WHEN GOD'S BEST IS BITTER

The king of Egypt said to the Hebrew midwives,
whose names were Shiphrah and Puah, "When you help the
Hebrew women in childbirth and observe them on the delivery
stool, if it is a boy, kill him; but if it is a girl, let her live."

EXODUS 1:15–16

Extreme hopes are born of extreme misery.

BERTRAND RUSSELL

*Y*ou know this story. The Egyptian Pharaoh was attempting to kill all the male Hebrew babies. How often have we read this text and focused so intently on the destruction designed to wipe out the masculine seed that we never noticed the last few words: "But if it is a girl, let her live."

As we glance backwards through the window of time, we see the female babies freed to live. What a start. What a frightful way to enter into the stream of life—with the possibility of death staring you in the face. Seconds away from a possible execution, a beautiful female soul is born.

Some of you, at your very genesis, began to experience fear and rejection. Maybe not this extreme, but rejection of any sort is unpleasant. You probably were not born under the threat of death, but perhaps you were not a planned child and entered this world uninvited. Maybe shortly after you arrived, you perceived that you were not welcome, not wanted. In your psyche, stored somewhere in the deep recesses of your soul, is that knowledge. You've probably felt like a misfit all of your life and experience an ongoing struggle to connect with others. You may long to become like everyone around you, but you never truly feel accepted as a member of the "in crowd."

Although you've experienced many bitter circumstances from your conception until now, you are in the exact place for which God designed you. You are meant to stand out. You are marked with a distinction that sets you apart from others and makes you steer differently through this world.

> YOU ARE IN THE EXACT PLACE FOR WHICH
> GOD DESIGNED YOU.

So often I watch godly Christian women who are confused about their dilemmas—about why they are suffering. I want to explain to them, "Everything is okay. You are right on point. God has everything that pertains to you under His control." But obviously I can't make myself heard to the many women who do not see clearly God's higher design for their lives.

Perhaps through these writings, you will begin to examine your own life and measure yourself by God's standards and not by the world's. Each struggle you encounter, each bitter place you pass through, is designed to bring you, as a Trophy Woman, to your full brilliance. We've noted that the tools God allows and uses are not always pleasant, yet they are necessary to make us into precious and special trophies.

IS GOD ANGRY WITH ME?

I don't remember how many years it took me to realize that God was not angry with me. Every time something went awry, each time a problem arose, I was certain that God was penalizing me for some sin. I actually felt I had to watch my steps each and every day, and I held my breath, hoping that I didn't get God upset with me. It took me some time to realize that the work Christ did on Calvary was once and for all. I had to examine the Scriptures meticulously to finally arrive at the conclusion that He came and died for me that I might have life.

Somehow I had gotten it backwards. I was a believer, but I believed that He came to see if I could live a perfect life. My life was guilt-ridden, because I knew I was a failure and unable to please Him. It was such a relief to finally realize that

if I could have lived spotlessly, it wouldn't have been necessary for Him to suffer and die as He did. It gave me great pleasure when His light dawned upon my soul, reminding me that He loves me and He came to make me free.

What you don't know *can* hurt you. Have you gone through so much trouble that you are certain that God is punishing you for your existence? We must stop persistently overlooking the Scripture that says: "Let us draw near to God with a sincere heart in full assurance of faith, having our hearts sprinkled to cleanse us from a guilty conscience and having our bodies washed with pure water. Let us hold unswervingly to the hope we profess, for he who promised [to forgive us] is faithful" (Heb. 10:22–23). If we have sought His forgiveness, ladies, *we have it* (1 John 1:9).

The afflictions, the sorrow, and the suffering are sometimes a part of the God-ordered steps for your life. It is confusing when you are a born-again believer and yet life continues to leave you clinging by your fingernails to the edge of darkness. It is confusing because we live in a generation of churchgoers who judge their right standing with God by how little trials are part of their lives. But God uses a higher and a different standard by which to measure the quality of our lives.

MEET A TROPHY WOMAN: MARY WASHINGTON

Take, for example, the story of Mary Washington, now a member of my church in Dallas, Texas. Here you have a woman who was a born-again Christian, living and doing the things she believed God would have her do. But in the middle of a move to Dallas, she and her husband, Jessie, fell on extremely hard times. While in the process of relocating, they had a car wreck, and after a series of events, they found themselves homeless. That's right. Both Mary and Jessie had been diligent, God-fearing parents of three children—one is mentally challenged—and then they were homeless.

> MARY AND JESSIE HAD BEEN DILIGENT,
> GOD-FEARING PARENTS OF THREE CHILDREN—
> AND THEN THEY WERE HOMELESS.

Mary learned adversity early. She is the youngest of four children. When she was eight years of age, her parents divorced, and she and her brothers and sisters were divided up between relatives. Mary was bounced around from house to house until she was sixteen years old.

She says today she never felt that she belonged anywhere and got along better with older people than with children her own age. She knows her disruptive childhood produced the anxiety she had to cope with as an adult.

Finally Mary married Jessie, a man who is a hard worker and who loves God. She watched him walk through the snow to buy groceries. He sold copper to supplement a dwindling income. But seventeen years into her marriage to a man who treated her well and tried to give his family the world, Mary found herself living in a car with her hus-

band and three children. The toughest of times were upon them.

But God had been shaping Mary's life from her child-hood; He had prepared her to survive this experience. She was fiercely determined to keep the family together. As the mother of a Down syndrome child, she had already seen God do the miraculous with her baby. The doctors had said her daughter would never walk, but she watched one night as her husband began to pray and call forth strength into the wobbly legs of their twelve-month-old. From that day forward, the little girl began to stand and later to walk.

As the years passed, Mary saw time after time that God came to their rescue with their little daughter. As God strengthened the child, He strengthened Mary's faith for the times to come.

Mary used the faith she had gained to help her through the homeless ordeal. She and her family lived for a time with a sister in her two-bedroom apartment, but with the additional five people in Mary's family, it was just too crowd-ed. The Washingtons finally had to use what was left of an insurance settlement from the wreck to pay for a hotel. When those finances were depleted, they opted to stay in the car rather than inconvenience relatives.

Mary says she will never forget using outdoor outlets to iron their clothes on park benches and washing their bod-ies in gas-station bathrooms. They parked their car near lighted areas so they would be safe through the nights. The irony of it all is that Jessie sang this whole time on The

Potter's House Praise Team, and no one in the entire church knew what the family was enduring. All anyone ever saw on Mary's face was a beautiful smile. (She was as courageous as the midwives we read about at the beginning of the chapter, Shiphrah and Puah!)

Finally when Jessie landed a job with The Potter's House ministry, he and Mary began to save money so they could find an apartment and move out of the car. How many people do you know who would silently endure such circumstances? The couple never complained, never uttered insults against the church—as many people do when they fall on hard times. In fact, it was after God had delivered them out of their trial that at a Sunday night service, Jessie sang a solo. Before he sang, he shared his testimony of what they had been through and how God brought them out. There wasn't a dry eye in the place while he sang "Great Is the Lord."

Mary Washington's discernment and ability to stand in the midst of a trial reminds me of Abigail. The Bible says that Abigail was a wise and beautiful woman (1 Sam. 25). Abigail's husband, Nabal, was a foolish, crabby man who invited trouble when he insulted King David and his men. Mary Washington's husband, Jessie, was neither a fool nor mean and stubborn, but he too was a man in trouble—a man who needed a strong, intelligent wife by his side. Abigail took matters into her owns hands to save her household by humbly appealing to David on her husband's behalf.

In the same way, Mary Washington took control of her emotions and calmly walked through a desert place, making her husband and children as comfortable as possible while they lived in the car. One thing she did specifically for Jessie was organize the towels and clothing in the trunk of the car so that he experienced as little disorder and confusion as she could arrange. As Mary kept the family's lives smooth and uncluttered, Jessie was free to spend his energy on fixing the problem. "Whoso findeth a wife findeth a good thing" (Prov. 18:22 KJV). That good thing is a Trophy Woman who is the handiwork of God.

Mary Washington refused to kill her marriage with her attitude. She refused to kill her husband with her mouth. She withstood the onslaught of bad circumstances against her family and saw the good in the man she married. Mary believed their covenant of marriage to be higher, more binding than the trial they were experiencing.

> MARY WASHINGTON REFUSED TO KILL
> HER MARRIAGE WITH HER ATTITUDE.

Imagine with me that your husband has you sleeping in a car with the kids, washing up in service stations, and going to church on Sunday morning to sing in the choir. Would you be able to hold your peace? How many women would have quietly complied? You have to be made from a substance of such supreme resiliency that only the hand of God could craft such a shining individual. Mary is an example to many women of how to stand by your man, walk alongside of him in the worst of times, and keep smiling in the face of sheer poverty and confusion.

What an extraordinary woman of God! Because she allowed God to make her and mold her through the situation, today Mary still has a strong, loving marriage. She and Jessie and the kids now reside in their own home. Yes, Mary experienced a severe time of testing, but she passed her test with flying colors. This remarkable lady always beams and exemplifies a quiet, triumphant faith we need to see more of today.

WHEN IT IS IMPOSSIBLE TO GIVE UP

God wants His women to be extraordinary so that we might show others how to navigate calmly through this dark world. You see, in spite of all the education and knowledge that freely abound today, the things we learn from experience are really the best teachers. And we can teach one another.

You may be living through a dark night of the soul—maybe not as severe as Mary Washington's, but nevertheless, it may seem that the odds are stacked against you. Often when life launches an attack on our souls, we want to run and hide. But sometimes, after we have become seasoned to conflict, trouble arrives and we refuse to perish. We come to a place where it is impossible to give up. We have too much to lose. It is a season to hold on and hold out.

> SOMETIMES, AFTER WE HAVE BECOME SEASONED TO
> CONFLICT, TROUBLE ARRIVES AND WE REFUSE TO PERISH.

You have walked the proving grounds of life. How bad do you want what you want: That marriage? That job? Your health? The finances or the relationship? Once we are faced with the challenges of life, we believers must do what we have been born again to do: believe.

Violently, savagely believe to see the promises of God fulfilled in your life and in your particular circumstances. Failure takes place only when you do not act upon what you know is within your power to perform. Believing the impossible and defying the odds are necessary to access your dream. Like Abigail and most certainly Mary Washington, believe and be bold. Be defiant enough to press your way through a bad situation to the best days of your life. You know that now is not the time to faint. Remember your status as a woman who is blessed and highly favored. Align your will with God for the highest and the most rewarding life.

Believe that though God's best may temporarily seem bitter, it will work for your best. Keep the faith, because help is just around the corner.

WHEN SHEER GALL IS REQUIRED

Let's look at two biblical examples. What incredible women Puah and Shiphah were! We read that despite the king's edict to kill all male babies, the midwives "feared God and did not do what the king of Egypt had told them to do; they let the boys live" (Exod. 1:17). They defied the evil orders and chose to do what was right and honorable. Certainly they must have been terrified to go against the insidious instruction, but when life demands hard decisions, you must choose life. You must be as brave as these women. It took sheer gall to defy the orders of the royal court and let the male babies live.

These women refused to be used for evil purposes. The Hebrew midwives did not accept the wicked opportunity to turn against their own people, the people with whom they were in covenant with God. It is similar to Mary Washington's decision to refuse to violate her covenant with her husband, Jessie. Mary and the midwives chose honor over self-preservation. They chose to love instead of hate.

Trophy Woman, you are the girl child whom God allowed to live. Live. Live well.

He lets you live for a good reason.

THAT WAS THEN . . .

Sometimes we need to do something tangible to move us from dark times in the direction of our dreams. There are numerous ways to begin to ease into our futures if we are in undesirable places.

> SOMETIMES WE NEED TO DO SOMETHING TANGIBLE
> TO MOVE US FROM DARK TIMES IN THE
> DIRECTION OF OUR DREAMS.

I remember my daughter saying, "Momma, let's take pictures of this old house. We won't live here forever." How I wish I had heeded her requests. Depression can sometimes seduce us into believing lies. I had become so discouraged in my low places that I did not want any records or evidence to remind me of them. To me, it was unthinkable to take pictures.

Today, I think differently. The seasons of our experiences make up who we are. If you are living in unsuitable housing, are currently in a hospital room, or are suffering from loss, get your camera and photograph every area of your life that you are praying for God to change. Put the pictures in a little photo book and write on the cover: *That Was Then*. In the second half of the book, write: *And This Is Now!* You may wait years to place your new pictures in the second half of the book, but the very act of believing that your current state will change will move you in the direction you desire to go.

We must always look ahead. The best really is yet to come. We are in the care of a loving Shepherd and Savior.

All of us, when going through a dark place, a scary time, a season of uncertainty, have wondered how we would manage to survive. You may be enduring such a time today. If the Lord is your Shepherd, it is His responsibility to guide you safely through the rough terrains, the jagged and narrow cliffs of life. Jesus is present to gently wipe the tears of life from your weeping eyes. Do not let your intense battle deceive you; all is well in the Master's hand. It is in His intense care that you experience His love and become acquainted with your personal Savior.

I remember being too physically, mentally, and emotionally weak to do anything but lay my weary soul upon His shoulders. It was in resting on Him that I found Him to be an excellent and divine Support System. I went through days, weeks, months, and even years only to realize that He was carrying me through my night seasons and leading me out into the glorious light.

Your struggle may be so severe that you are out of options. Do not worry. Rest in Him; rely upon Him. He is leading you, Trophy Woman, along life's perilous highway. He is more than willing and able to bring you out of whatever valley you may be facing.

He will bring you out. He brought me.

Turning Point

It has taken Time
To reconstruct
My struggle
And to persuade
My darkness to
Peel back the black
Skin of the night sky
Expressly to reveal
This unbroken
Sea of Light.

Questions for Reflection

❦ *Have you ever felt as though God were angry with you? How did you handle that feeling—by withdrawing from Him and other believers, or by drawing closer?*

❦ *If you were in Mary Washington's shoes, could you have withstood homelessness without wounding your loved ones with words? What would be hardest for you in that situation?*

❦ *Have you experienced a dark night of the soul—in which you found it impossible to give up? If so, what kept you going? If not, how can you bolster your faith for future difficulties?*

❦ *"Trophy Woman, you are the girl child whom God allowed to live. Live well." How can you do this?*

❦ *What tangible thing can you do to move yourself in the direction of your dreams? Consider Jacqueline's idea of* "That Was Then" *and* "This Is Now" *photographs.*

 Prayer

Father God,

We honor You today with praise and thanksgiving. As we approach Your throne, we are reminded that there is none like You and none above You, and for this we are grateful. We reach for You, knowing that we have come to the pinnacle of life—Alpha and Omega, the Highest of the most high. What a privilege to have relationship with You, my Lord, my Savior, and my King.

Today, Lord, I lift my sister up to You. Please breathe into her life and let her feel the sweetness of Your presence. Do something special for her today. We know that You've already performed the greatest deed anyone could ever do: You died for her. And because You loved her enough to die for her, please remind her of Your unfailing love by soothing her situation with Your presence. Stand up in her life, God, and let her have full confidence in You. Let her be an eyewitness to your Your ability to ease the tensions within and to lighten her heavy burdens.

Provide this woman the urgent care she needs. Halt the heartbreaking moments that attempt to overwhelm her. Replace her misery with hope, comfort, and joy. Do those things that will leave her undeniably indebted to You with her love. Let Your peace and grace reign supreme in her life. I praise You, Lord, for the immediate relief coming to my sister.

In Jesus' name, amen.

6

THE TREASURES OF DARKNESS

*I will give you the treasures of darkness, riches stored
in secret places, so that you may know that I am the LORD,
the God of Israel, who summons you by name.*

ISAIAH 45:3

Look at this powerful Scripture. Wow! Those of you who have experienced a season of testing, who have experienced any kind of intense trial, can bear witness with me that you came forth with hidden treasures locked deep inside your secret places. God's Trophy Women never come up empty after enduring a season of distress.

Webster's defines *treasure* as "something of great worth or value."[1] So what do I mean by *hidden treasures*? You are probably familiar with the old saying, "I wouldn't take nothing for my journey." Does that mean you would want to go through those arduous testing times again? Heavens no! But

I wouldn't trade what I know from those experiences for anything—would you?

Christians say that we must have a personal relationship with Jesus, and that is so true. But many people are not aware that they can be born-again believers yet still not know Jesus as Lord. Yes, they made their confession of faith and day by day, they live by faith. But that kind of passion-less Christian is totally different from the believer who has had to cling to Him desperately to rescue her from some-thing horrific. I place tremendous value on the women who have walked with God through something sinister and come out of it to tell the rest of us that we can make it, that Jesus is Lord, and that nothing is too hard for God.

It is one thing to lean over to your church neighbor dur-ing the Sunday service and say, "God can do anything." It's a completely different matter to know, within the very recesses of your soul, that He *can* do *anything* because you have been the eyewitness to the great things He has done for you—you have experienced His blessing and favor!

> IT'S A COMPLETELY DIFFERENT MATTER TO KNOW,
> WITHIN THE VERY RECESSES OF YOUR SOUL,
> THAT HE <u>CAN</u> DO <u>ANYTHING</u>.

Not long ago, I watched a woman on TV share her account of a life-threatening illness. There she sat during her interview, smiling, saying that she had never entertained the idea of not surviving. I was surprised at her nonchalance. Can we judge another person's response to illness? Of course not. We are warned in the Bible not to judge another man's servant (Rom. 14:4). But I couldn't help wondering why she had not reaped more from her adversity.

Seemingly the experience had not changed any portion of her life; she made her ordeal sound as if it were just another occurrence in her life experience, not an extraordinary challenge that had demanded intense struggle. Perhaps she chose not to share this information with her audience. But inside, I hoped that her experience had made her a better woman, a stronger woman, and that she had not gone through those turbulent times only to return to her everyday existence untouched and unchanged.

"Make Happy"?

When we undergo any kind of anguish or suffering, our assignment is not to put on a fake face and smile as if nothing has happened. We are obligated to report back a sincere account of our experience, and that will include an ending where God gets the glory. Surely we do not want to give impure and partial accounts where we are perceived as the heroine. No. It is God who must get the glory from our lives. When He gets the glory, the tribute, and the recognition, we shine. To appear invincible makes us unhelpful to our fellow sisters who suffer the loss of their health, their spouses, their children, or their waning lives.

I realize we live in a society that promotes the appearance

of wellness without the reality of wholeness. Ours is a society that teaches people to "make happy" and appear at ease at all times: give the public an image of perfection throughout deaths, wars, and destruction. Our culture requires, even applauds, its citizens who put on a happy face so that no one will think they are weak, complaining, or negative. But it is dishonest to feign supremacy when only God is indestructible and only God is preeminent. The reality is that if God had not been on this woman's side, her disease would have swallowed her up. Why she didn't say so, I will not judge.

(Let me add that Mary Washington, whom you met in the last chapter, wasn't like those who pretend to glide through problems. She didn't smile and beam throughout her ordeal because she was "making happy"—Mary's joy was real. She stayed connected to her Creator, and He made sure she shined.)

THE GREATER THE DARKNESS, THE GREATER THE NEED—AND THE DELIVERANCE

I have never felt the presence of the Lord as keenly as when I needed Him desperately to heal my broken soul and body. You know how it is when you are driving a car and you need more power? I am from the hills of West Virginia, where steep hills and mountainsides are everywhere. While you are driving in the valleys, or hollows as they are known there, you need only one gear, but when you start to ascend into the mountains, you can hear your car kick into another gear.

It is the same when you walk with God through the valley of the shadow of death. God gives you mountaintop driving in the deep, dark valleys of your life. He doesn't kick in for your normal day-to-day living the way He does when you are in trouble. God does not reveal the arsenals of heaven when you simply need a parking space. Find your own parking spot. When you get in trouble, when you have a grave affliction, when you are the loneliest, those are the times when you can feel His nearness, sense His carrying you through places where no one can help you. It is in these places and in these times that you experience His power, His might, and His miracles.

GOD DOES NOT REVEAL THE ARSENALS OF HEAVEN
WHEN YOU SIMPLY NEED A PARKING SPACE.

The treasures found in your dark places contain your intimate knowledge of God. Those are the hidden riches you know only from having had to lean on Him, call on Him, and believe Him. You are privy to the heart of God.

You don't really know a person until you go through something with him. A long-lasting marriage is so precious because the two people have been through many challenges together. So it is in our relationship with the Lord.

When two people first marry, they are so cute. They are certain that no matter what comes, they will always feel the same affection they felt at the altar. We look at the happy couple and everyone is in their corner. We are rooting for

them. We want the best for them. But you and I know their their love and commitment have yet to be tested. They cannot fathom the many, many times their relationship will be tried in the fires of life.

The beginning of marriage is not the time to write a book about relationships. We wouldn't respect the words and advice of newlyweds. We realize that without a proven period of time together, this husband and wife don't have much credibility. Why? Because they don't know what they will do, feel, or become until time and adversity have proven their love to be strong and lasting.

To heed the advice of someone who has not been tested is like taking life lessons and instruction from a two-year-old. Who would take to heart the guidance of a child?

No, we need counsel from those who have endured the crises of life—other Trophy Women. We need comfort from God, who cares deeply about His women. And I am a witness: the more broken the soul, the more thorough His relief.

Sweet Victory!

As God crafts us into the trophies He wishes to see, He takes us through processes and procedures that are baffling and breathtaking. Sometimes we feel as if God is trying to kill us! But when we finally emerge from the steam bath of life, and before we are plunged into the next smelting pot, something in us remembers: He was faithful over the past difficulties, and we can count on Him to be faithful in our futures. Extreme tests may visit us until one day, it dawns on our precious minds that trusting Him in the darkness brings comfort, relief, and peace. God has already taught you spiritual warfare. He has brought you through too many difficult situations for you to panic this time.

> HE TAKES US THROUGH PROCESSES AND PROCEDURES
> THAT ARE BAFFLING AND BREATHTAKING.

Because God has delivered you so often, you know about Him not from a book but from experience. I am a little concerned for the women who have yet to walk through dark places with Him, only because they haven't explored the depths of their relationship with God. They don't yet know that He will sustain them in extraordinary ways. They've not watched Him bring water out of a rock when they walk through a desert of life. They have yet to fully realize that He'll be whatever they need Him to be, so their faith is untried—and often unstable.

My faith became strong only after it was tested. When my marriage failed, I had to struggle to make ends meet as a single parent. The things God did to bless my life were amazing. But in order to receive the blessing, I had to trust Him, to call upon Him.

I will never forget a particularly challenging time when I was calling on the Lord. One day I found a one-hundred-dollar bill in a little decorative can sitting on top of my

dresser. At that time, it was a great deal of money. To this date, I do not remember putting the money aside, though surely I must have, but it certainly appeared when I needed it. God must have nudged me to tuck it away for a rainy day, but all of those days were rainy. Nevertheless, the money was there to pay a phone bill before a cutoff could take place. I rejoiced.

I know you too have numerous stories to tell about when God has blessed your life with unexplainable answers to prayer. I can't help but share one other story with you about God's sustaining power and His amazing grace. Many, many years ago, I worked for a company that paid very little. My paycheck barely covered the necessities. But one day the employees received a memo saying that an agency would reevaluate each position in the company. We were told to write up our job descriptions.

Do you know that the company that would not promote me, would not give me a raise, received a mandate from the head of the agency to increase my salary by three thousand dollars? While others around me were demoted or kept at the same pay levels, my salary was increased without debate or controversy, and it was irrevocable! I was one happy woman. Hallelujah! Thank You, Jesus! Glory to God! Praise God! I drove home from work that night riding on a cloud, shouting and praising God! The battle was not mine, but the Lord's. Sweet victory!

The treasure lies in discovering that God is *for* each of us, personally. Yes, He loves us collectively. Yes, He loves the body of Christ, but when you realize that He personally loves *you,* it is exhilarating.

WE *NEVER* SUFFER ALONE

One of the treasures in the darkness is knowing that God hears our prayers. Another treasure is knowing that He will make a way out of no way. Another treasure is knowing that I am His friend and for that reason I am not someone to vex—God likes to hear me laugh and to see me smile. Another treasure is knowing that God is present in every part of my life. He appears where others cannot go, especially in times of trouble.

God is in your subconscious and He is present when you are unconscious. In the darkness, He is the treasure that you will find faithful, waiting, solidly present, and available to you. He is there when you experience trouble others cannot fathom. God, who is rich in mercy, waits on you when you hit rock bottom, when you find yourself in the hard, dark places of life. He is with you in the midst of the anguish. He is what you find in your darkness.

Trophy Women, it is in your human struggle, your life experience, that you are invited to share your drama, your heartbreak, your loss, your worries, your fears, your pain, and your affliction with God. It is in the pain that you discover what "blessed and highly favored" really means. You don't begin to know the wealth of God—the mercy, kindness, and comfort of God—until you go through the darkness. It

is then that you begin to see how blessed you are to be His child.

I can hear someone say, "Well, all people struggle and suffer." You are right. But suffering *with* Him, including Him in every aspect of our lives, is what matters. Scripture tells us that Jesus is able "to sympathize with our weaknesses" (Heb. 4:15). Clinging to Christ in our suffering is the secret to getting the most out of our adversity.

> SUFFERING <u>WITH</u> HIM, INCLUDING HIM IN EVERY ASPECT OF OUR LIVES, IS WHAT MATTERS.

Reaping the goodness of God comes from taking Him into your tragedy. By inviting Him to walk with you through the darkness, you begin to know that no matter how painful, how discouraging, and how hopeless your situation, God can turn it around. You get to watch Him show up and show out for you. You get to watch Him order your steps and resolve impossible situations on your behalf. You will no longer have head knowledge of Jesus, but heart knowledge of a risen, vibrant, and faithful Savior.

MEET A TROPHY WOMAN: JUANITA SAPP

My friend, evangelist Juanita Sapp, is someone who knows firsthand the mercy, provision, and healing of the Lord. She has traveled with Him through many dark and dangerous places. I've seen her pushed in her wheelchair to the front of the church to attend Sunday service. She has always been dressed in something wonderful and looked radiant. I asked if I could share her testimony with my readers and she agreed to let me showcase her life.

Juanita was twenty-three years old when her ankles started to bother her. She went to many doctors but received no diagnosis. One morning after she turned twenty-four, the middle knuckle of her left hand was red, swollen, and very painful. She again began the trips to the doctors, who said that she had arthritis. Later the disease spread to the right hand, but at that time she still had the strength to keep moving. By the time she turned thirty-eight, she was wheelchair-bound and required pain medication to function. All of the medications for arthritis that worked for most people produced overwhelming side effects, and one almost took her life.

Juanita has wrestled with this disease for thirty-two years. Her toes are terribly deformed and her hands are gnarled and twisted. But before and since this crippling disease struck her life, Juanita has served the Lord. If you had the opportunity to speak with her, she would tell you that just as God called the light out of darkness in the book of Genesis, He will call light from your darkness to illuminate your life. His light, she says, enlightens and gives knowledge: "And God said, Let there be light: and there was light. And God saw the light, that it was good: and God divided the light from the darkness" (Gen. 1:3–4 KJV).

God sparked light in darkness for Juanita. Today, she is

out of the wheelchair. After two knee-replacement surgeries, she is able to walk. It is wonderful just to see her enter a room. She ministers the word of God around the country and is a beautiful and faithful servant of the Lord.

TREASURE FROM TRAVAIL

Juanita would agree: you and I never activate the strength within until we are called upon to do so. The Lord is our Strength. Yes, the test is grievous, but it is a powerful revelator too.

> YOU AND I NEVER ACTIVATE THE STRENGTH WITHIN UNTIL WE ARE CALLED UPON TO DO SO.

An abundance of hidden riches is found in the midst of travail. I was blessed with a good mother and was fortunate enough to see the value of good parenting early in my life. Though I knew the importance of conscientious and supportive mothering, I achieved my dream to pay special attention to my parenting skills through my illness. My medical challenges allowed me the opportunity to become the excellent mother I envisioned.

Despite sickness, or perhaps because of it, it was imperative to me that I train my daughter to see the Lord in every good gift we received. I was meticulous about her care and her little life. Although she was aware, the way all bright little children are, that things were out of sorts in our house, I was careful to teach her to recognize the hand of the Lord, to point out to her His deliverance and provision. From her childhood, she has learned to be grateful and to celebrate His presence.

When in trouble, people do not live carelessly. Those things that are important are not neglected or put aside. It was many, many years later that my daughter said, "Momma, do you realize that you put me into a private Christian school, participated in every part of my life, attended every school and social function where I was involved, and you did it all while you were ill?" I honestly had never noticed. To me, it was mandatory that I guide my child into relationship with the Lord and to solidify her emotionally, spiritually, and physically to the best of my ability. Shakespeare said it well: "Sweet are the uses of adversity."

In the world of the twenty-first century, we are so trained to want quick fixes and easy answers to our problems. But God does not always develop us with microwave solutions. Subliminally, we try to keep up the image that our lives are flawless, but that is almost never the case.

Let me say something shocking to many of you: looking good can sometimes be the last thing you want. Yes, I said it. Sometimes you can have it too good! Let me explain what I mean. So many times the woman who has the image of perfection goes unnoticed. She goes unattended. But the woman who subtly—without attempting to draw attention to herself—shows signs of wear and tear, distress and fatigue, gets attention.

LOOKING GOOD CAN SOMETIMES BE
THE LAST THING YOU WANT.

You've seen that tired, frazzled single mom rushing her children to Sunday school so that she can go into the main sanctuary for service. She is working hard to be a great role model and to guide her children correctly. An extreme example is that bag woman you see underneath the highway overpass. Don't you utter a prayer for her? I am sure you sometimes stop and put money into her hand or say a kind word to her. She caught your attention because of her severe living condition. Little children who are poorly dressed catch your eye too.

People who are in trouble, uncared for and in distress, are usually easy to spot. Their trouble is so apparent that it jolts us to attention. Most of us women are natural nurturers, moved emotionally by suffering, and our hearts are pulled when we see misery. God is moved by our plight as well, as we can see in the life of Leah: "And [Jacob] . . . loved also Rachel more than Leah. . . . And when the LORD saw that Leah was hated, he opened her womb: but Rachel was barren" (Gen. 29:30–31 KJV).

God moved on Leah's behalf *because* she was hated. Her extreme condition caught His attention and caused Him to bless her. Leah found favor in the darkness. In the midst of rejection by man, she found acceptance and blessing with God.

Now, I'm not suggesting that you walk around looking

shabby or depressed—just that you be transparent enough to admit you are stressed and waiting on God to deliver you. Others who have walked the same road can empathize and help you along.

The challenge that you, my sister, currently face today may usher you into the very presence of God so that He may reveal the biggest blessings of your life: treasure in the darkness, the provision and the blessing of the Lord.

STARS FOR SCARS

I recall my own situation nearly twenty-two years ago. I was a born-again believer, but when one Sunday morning my brother preached a message entitled "May I Have Your Attention, Please?" I went home and sobbed my eyes out. I wept because my spirit knew what my mind could not perceive. God was calling me into a deeper relationship with Him, and my tears foretold the darkness and severity of the journey to come.

Little did I know what was about to happen—that next morning was the beginning of a new world for me.

I went to work as usual. To my amazement, later that morning I woke up in a hospital. I had collapsed while working and had been physically carried by a coworker to get help and then rushed to a nearby hospital. Quite understandably, I was alarmed. I had been perfectly healthy, I thought, and had no symptoms that suggested anything of this magnitude might occur. One test led to other tests until

finally, I was told that I had a tumor in my brain and it was growing.

One Sunday message, a medical crisis at work: six months later, I lay on a table, a young lady surrounded by doctors and equipment and prepped to undergo brain surgery that would last eight hours. Eight hours! The surgeons untangled arteries and veins and my entire life changed. I've mentioned that for ten years I struggled to recover from this difficult event.

Trophy Women, weeping may endure for the night, but joy cometh in morning. My night lasted nearly a decade. It took me so long to return to normal that I did not speak about or give intimate details of my journey back to health until many years later. God gave me strength for the days to come and for the process He allowed me to endure.

From my scars, God gave me stars of hope from His Word to light my path and guide me slowly along His chosen direction for my life. When God forms you, He fashions you slowly, delicately, and skillfully. He masterfully leads you to ensure that you are forever His—to ensure that your radiance is all anyone can see.

Once you emerge from a place of isolation and trial, you realize it was actually a gift handed to you in strange wrappings. No, it is certainly not the kind of present anyone desires or would ever ask to receive, but when you glance back at your experience and see what God accomplished in your life, when you examine the fine vessel you've become, it is startling to see how much good He brings from tragedy.

Let me be very clear about suffering. I am not a proponent of, or one who enjoys, misery, nor do I support self-flagellation. But I do know the Scriptures say to take up our crosses and follow Him: "And anyone who does not take his cross and follow me is not worthy of me" (Matt. 10:38). Clearly, God has called us to face troubles just as Jesus did.

Look at this Scripture: "And there came a voice from heaven, saying, Thou art my beloved Son, in whom I am well pleased. And immediately the spirit driveth him into the wilderness" (Mark 1:11–12 KJV). Mark says that the Spirit drove Jesus into the wilderness. Why? The Scripture tells us He pleased God, yet He was driven into the wilderness and tested. Wow! The thought that we too may have wilderness experiences because we please God is baffling, but our faith is tested to prove us and to reveal that we are His. God's love and care look funny sometimes, but He who began a good work in us is able to perform it to the day of redemption. He has a plan for our lives.

WHAT TREASURES WE GLEAN

In my humble estimation, it is impossible to gain treasures from suffering when we create the suffering ourselves. We must trust that God's hand is on the thermostat of our fiery furnaces; we must wholly have faith in Him. The darkness and the unfamiliar make us keep our hands tightly in God's. Jesus is the only way out of our night season. And once we arrive in the light, sometimes much later, we recognize the

gift of having had an unexpected walk through the valley of the shadow of death. The gift is that we see life as more precious, more enjoyable, and less intimidating. We begin to live our lives anew.

And, although we now have a great appreciation for the frailty of life, the euphoria we experience once we come through all those difficult situations victoriously is delicious, breathtaking, humbling, and empowering, all in one sweep.

Scripture tells us that after we have suffered awhile, God makes us mature: He "will himself restore [us] and make [us] strong" (1 Pet. 5:10). He causes us to see life from a perspective of sobriety. When we've passed through a life-changing experience, we do not have to be taught what matters. We now know! The ability to discern what is significant in this life is a treasure from the darkness.

Affliction causes us to focus only on what matters. We are rigorously reminded that this fallen world is not our home. We are passing through and heaven-bound. Because the beauty of this earth seduces us, we often attempt to transform this fallen world into our home. It is not. Adversity gives the correct perspective: this world is a passageway to our eternal heavenly home. We remember this as God develops our faith and urges us, through our life experiences, to keep our eyes and hearts heavenward.

We read in Colossians: "Since, then, you have been raised with Christ, set your hearts on things above, where Christ is seated at the right hand of God. Set your minds on things above, not on earthly things. For you died, and your life is now hidden with Christ in God" (3:1–3). As we seek those things from above, when our perspective is adjusted, suddenly we don't have time for foolishness. We move about, taking care of what is near and dear to our hearts: our health, our families, and our relationships.

When we face losing anything of value, immediately we become focused, like the light of a laser beam, only on those areas of significance. Silly, irritating things are of no consequence now—not when we face a life-threatening illness, not when our only son joined the service in the middle of a war, not when that twenty-five-year marriage starts to quickly slide down the drain and into a divorce court, not when our company is downsizing and we are unprepared for any other position or retirement.

> WHEN OUR PERSPECTIVE IS ADJUSTED, SUDDENLY
> WE DON'T HAVE TIME FOR FOOLISHNESS.

Now our senses are keen as we strain to hear the voice and the direction of the Lord. We realize now more than ever our sincere need for God. Now we are intensely aware that we cannot make it through this world without Him. The ministry of trouble gets our attention and drives us straight into the arms of God. Like the aggravating grain of sand embedded inside the oyster's shell, exasperating situations are rubbing against the lining of our delicate lives, bringing us into the presence of God. And, just as the oyster that turns the sand into a priceless and precious pearl, God is

using the trials of our lives to polish our faith and to make us trophies. Now we understand clearly the Jewish proverb: "Light is not recognized except through darkness."

Treasures in the darkness are the secrets revealed to those who have been made symbols of excellence through some extraordinary set of circumstances. How amazing and clever for God to hide His riches in darkness. Who would think to look for gifts in the night seasons of life? But that is exactly where God has stashed them.

> HOW AMAZING AND CLEVER FOR GOD
> TO HIDE HIS RICHES IN DARKNESS.

Finally, we begin to see a loving God who wants our fellowship and our undivided attention. Through our human struggles, we are made to humble ourselves under His mighty hand, that in due season He might exalt us to a higher and more desirable position—reveal us as women who are blessed and highly favored—and thereby allow us to make a difference in someone else's life.

FELLOWSHIP OF THE BROKEN

Since my personal experience with the Lord, I am attracted to people whom God has broken and blessed. These are women who belong to a secret society of kingdom living. The women I know who have undergone long passages through dark places have emerged as fine vessels. They are the trophies that shine so brightly. They are symbols of excellence. You can quickly identify women who have been students of suffering; they emerge from their struggles with boundless wisdom. Because affliction has given them expert vision and spiritual awakening, these women are delighted to have "life and live more abundantly."

Here are women who are not puzzled or perplexed by everyday living. Are they models of perfection? Are they without faults? No. But they are remarkable women whose times of testing have softened their hearts, brightened their attitudes, and made them useful in God's kingdom.

Ladies, these are not words to romanticize the hard times. These are words of truth to encourage you as you face your darkest night—the season that will change you into an entirely spectacular handiwork of the Master.

Godly women are in the hands of a loving, merciful, and kind God. If He has allowed or ordered some strange, unusually harsh conditions for you, please remember He is with you in the night: "Dear friends, do not be surprised at the painful trial you are suffering, as though something strange were happening to you. But rejoice that you participate in the sufferings of Christ, so that you may be overjoyed when his glory is revealed" (1 Pet. 4:12–13). Although it doesn't appear that you will win or escape when you are tried in fiery furnaces of life, cling to the promise of deliverance—to the purpose of refinement. Remember that what goes into a furnace is not what comes out: you become God's masterpiece—a Trophy Woman.

Emerald Laughter

I watched as ribbons of laughter spun from her lips
Exposing the glimmer of hope now birthed in her eyes.

The sound devoured the air,
Like boiling clouds piling high in a Texas sky
Embracing the bystanders
Who marveled at the
Obvious angelic delight of a woman
Emerging
From the abyss
Radiating in the fresh, priceless triumph
Of knowing
Her struggle is now over.

Questions for Reflection

- *Do you know, within the depths of your soul, that God can do anything? What experiences have built this faith in you?*

- *Have you ever hidden your pain and "made happy" so others wouldn't know you were struggling? Why was that important?*

- *What baffling experiences has God taken you through?*

- *What treasures have you discovered in the darkness?*

- *Do you know a woman who has been a "student of suffering"? How did she endure?*

Father,

I thank You for allowing me to see firsthand Your extreme conditions and Your extreme deliverances.

Lord, I pray for my sister who has yet to know You as a mighty Deliverer and Anchor. Do for her those things only You can do: heal, deliver, and set her free. And Lord, open her eyes and understanding so she may know that You hold her life and all that pertains to her in Your mighty hand.

Bless this woman to relax in You and anoint her with the ability to have faith in You as You guide her safely through this life. Let her know with all confidence that what You've allowed in her life will only be used to make her an exceptional woman of Your master design.

In Jesus' name I pray, amen.

7

SPOTS, WRINKLES, AND BLEMISHES CAN TARNISH TROPHIES

That he might present it to himself a glorious church,
not having spot, or wrinkle or any such thing; but should
be holy and without blemish.

EPHESIANS 5:27 (KJV)

*I*n Ephesians 5, the apostle Paul discussed sin issues and preparing the body of Christ for how it, as His bride, will be presented: as a spotless, sinless, and unsoiled church.

The words *spots, wrinkles,* and *blemishes* remind me of the very thing I often hear both young and aging women discussing: we do not want to appear physically flawed. We want to have impeccable images. But the Word of God talks to us about having inner attributes far more important than our outer ones.

Our society touts the American ideal of beauty. We are constantly bombarded with advertisements that promote the latest cosmetic surgery. Don't get me wrong: I am in no way against looking good. I sincerely believe a woman should put her best foot forward as much as possible. To me, it is just part of our feminine behavior to look spectacular, to smell good, and to appear elegant as often as we can.

What I am talking about here is balance. Putting all of the emphasis on outer appearance is not only unhealthy, it is unwise. If all you are interested in developing and maintaining are your lips, hips, and fingertips, you are walking on very fragile and dreadfully shallow ground.

> IF ALL YOU ARE INTERESTED IN DEVELOPING
> AND MAINTAINING ARE YOUR LIPS, HIPS, AND
> FINGERTIPS, YOU ARE WALKING ON DREADFULLY
> SHALLOW GROUND.

Read with me 1 Peter 3:3–5:

Your beauty should not come from outward adornment, such as braided hair and the wearing of gold jewelry and fine clothes. Instead, it should be that of your inner self, the unfading beauty of a gentle and quiet spirit, which is of great worth in God's sight. For this is the way the holy women of the past who put their hope in God used to make themselves beautiful.

We don't want to ignore our physical appearance, but we don't want to place more value on the outer shell than on our inner world. As you walk with God through the years, age gracefully, knowing that your value is hidden within your earthen vessel. Accept changes in your body due to the laws of gravity. One day, this earthen vessel will completely disappear and reveal only your innermost being.

As God's Trophy Woman, you want to shine, brilliant and bright. The contents of your character are far more precious than any false identity hiding behind a face on the edge of collapse. No matter how much cosmetic work you have done (if pursued in moderation, there's nothing wrong with that), at some point you have to know that there is a limit and a danger zone.

Have you noticed how this world has a way of drawing unsuspecting, insecure women, especially those who have not been made over again by the Master's hand, into making decisions and maintaining attitudes that will not provide them with the lasting loveliness they so desire? Seek a better beauty.

Spots: Perceived Imperfections

I watched a terribly disturbing but helpful *Oprah* show one afternoon. She featured a group of women who were addicted to plastic surgery. Can you imagine a woman saying that if she could have a surgery every day to perfect her perceived imperfections, she would? I was aghast. What makes women

pursue unnecessary and drastic alterations to their bodies? Actually, none of these women had horrendous outward imperfections, but inwardly, monstrous problems were brewing.

Sadly, I watched some of the women crying and saying they wished they had never gotten started with their physical makeovers, because they found themselves trapped. They could not stop altering their appearance. Here were women who apparently suffer from an obsessive disorder: one surgery led them into the madness of cutting their bodies again and again.

Those women brought to my mind a possessed man whom Jesus healed: "And always, night and day, he was in the mountains, and in the tombs, crying, and cutting himself with stones" (Mark 5:5 KJV). This man needed a touch from Jesus. As I watched these miserable, afflicted women, I could not help but believe they sorely needed a beauty makeover from the inside out, which can come only from the hand of God. When you don't have a good sense of yourself, or worse, if you are unaware of your position in God, the relentless attempts to bring about inner change through bodily reconstruction and the mistaken beliefs concerning the self-image can be chilling.

Isn't it imperative that we see ourselves as God sees us? His vision is perfect. It is fruitless to follow the world's directives. Christ told us to be in this world but not of this world. He knew that the world would dictate principles and ideas that are empty and without meaning, but we are to live as blessed and highly favored women. He ordained better for us—if we will follow Him to get it.

The Beauty of Dusk

A few years ago, my precious grandson, Isaac, was playing on my balcony. I had taught him a new word a few days prior. I knew he remembered the word and its meaning when he began calling to me, "Nana! Nana! It's dusk." I smiled, so pleased that he used the word correctly. *Webster's* describes *dusk* as "the darker part of twilight," twilight being the period of time between sunset and full night.[1]

It may not quite be nighttime in your life, but it may be the darker part of the light. Society tries to convince us that at a certain age we are no more than fading beauties or tarnished trophies. But that is so far from the truth. Some of the best-kept secrets are the strengths, the wonders, and the treasures of growing older. You are *not* collecting dust and sitting on a shelf. You are *not* useless. You become more valuable with age and experience.

Think about it: whatever your age, if you have kept in step with the Savior, you know more about the Lord and your résumé with God has become quite extensive. You have teachings to share with others and your words now have weight and worth. What this world sees as a weathered woman is actually a symbol of victories past, a sign of accomplishment, and a testimony of glorious days. You are the perfect image of the handiwork of God.

You have what I call *wise woman beauty*. Your many seasons of testing have led you into a special position with God. You have lived through a myriad of situations, and because you trusted and walked hand-in-hand with a risen Savior, nothing has taken the warmth from your heart. Isn't your sense of freedom and strength wondrous?

Even if your body is beginning its downward flow, your spirit is getting stronger and now soars from the tremendous knowledge you possess. Not only are you certain that God hears your prayers, but others seek to hear your words and draw from your knowledge that they might more easily make their way through this world. Your wisdom makes you a lifesaver to many people. You are a queen and one of God's Trophy Women.

> **YOUR WISDOM MAKES YOU A LIFESAVER TO MANY PEOPLE.**

MEET A TROPHY WOMAN: LORENA GRAY

I am privileged to come from the ranks of some incredible, Bible-believing Trophy Women. Both Susie Patton, my mother's mom (whom I'll share with you later) and Lorena Gray, Daddy's mother, were courageous, strong, loving women. Although they met only once, they shared some wonderful similarities. Both ladies were servants to others.

They reached out to people in need: family members, neighbors, and people who simply passed through their lives.

Grandmother Lorena always had provisions for people. Food was an abundant commodity in her spotless home. She happily spread around the contents of her freezer and her gardens. My grandmother was known for sharing, supplying, and hard work.

She and her first husband, T. D. Jakes, lived in rural Mississippi. When my dad, Ernest, was very young, and while Grandmother was carrying her second child, her husband drowned in what appeared to be an accident. Later it was discovered that he had actually been murdered in the waters in which he swam each day. Everyone knew he was an excellent swimmer and he often swam the river to work rather than walk the road to his job. For some reason, none that could possibly explain such actions, my grandfather was warned not to continue this habit. Barbed wire was later found in the river on the watery pathway that led to the death of a strong man, a strong swimmer, a strong father and husband.

My grandmother did not let the death of her husband make her bitter, a racist, or a quitter. She continued to work on their farm, raise their children, and later married again. She didn't break under the pressure, she didn't question her belief in God, nor did she falter in her pursuit of excellence. Later when she was well into midlife she graduated from college, opened and directed a Head Start program for

needy children, and continued to be the point person in her community for help with food or other needs.

Don't you respect people who don't fold, who lean upon the strong arms of the Lord to carry them through the storms of life?

My grandmother Lorena had married very young, acquired a farm, and worked the land. She developed her farm so that she brought in additional income through crop sales; her work enabled her to purchase additional pieces of land. She was the kind of strong, vibrant woman who had witnessed sorrow and trouble, but because of her immovable belief in God, trouble did not take the smile from her heart or the joy from her dreams. She was a woman who was known for helping many people throughout her journey on this earth.

In her eighties, she once commented to my brother that she couldn't believe she was unable to drive her truck anymore. Her responses had slowed and her vision was becoming blurred. When her health began to fail, when life wouldn't bend for her, she bent for it. Growing old gracefully is an art that we must master with class as women of distinction. Grandma modeled this for me as one of God's Trophy Women.

MAKING THE MOST OF "DUSK"

The apostle Peter called those who follow Jesus "a chosen generation, a royal priesthood, an holy nation, a peculiar people" (1 Pet. 2:9 KJV). If we are to be "peculiar people," we might as well be so uncommon that we are seen leaving this world with smiles on our faces and a gleam in our eyes. As we grow nearer to our heavenly home, we must remind ourselves that in reality, you and I as believers are similar to celestial gypsies passing through this world to reach our divine destination. When you begin to see life as an earthly journey, it takes the sting out of bodily changes. You begin to understand that you are shedding this imperfect and limited shell to get dressed in heavenly glory.

> YOU AND I AS BELIEVERS ARE SIMILAR TO
> CELESTIAL GYPSIES PASSING THROUGH THIS
> WORLD TO REACH OUR DIVINE DESTINATION.

I certainly don't want to trivialize the aging process, but you know how we women love to get dressed up and look ravishing to go somewhere wonderful. We are like Cinderella who was dirty, tattered, and stained from the ashes of her existence: when her chance to change came, she dressed as the belle of the ball. Our transition from this life to the next will reveal our finest wear. What we possess on the inside is so much more splendid than anything this world has seen. Paul wrote,

I consider that our present sufferings are not worth comparing with the glory that will be revealed in us. The creation waits in eager expectation for the sons of God to be revealed. For the creation was subjected to frustration, not by its own choice, but by the will

of the one who subjected it, in hope that the creation itself will be liberated from its bondage to decay and brought into the glorious freedom of the children of God.

We know that the whole creation has been groaning as in the pains of childbirth right up to the present time. Not only so, but we ourselves, who have the firstfruits of the Spirit, groan inwardly as we wait eagerly for our adoption as sons, the redemption of our bodies. (Romans 8:18–23)

Young and old, we are all awaiting the end of decay. But we shouldn't underestimate what gifts aging brings. Some of my friends who are now in their seventies and eighties are lovely women. One recently shared with me: "In your fifties, you are a young woman and you are a seasoned woman. It is a wonderful time." It is important to listen to those who have gone where we are yet to go. Therefore, if you are a middle-aged beauty, forget "spots"—perceived imperfections. Now is the time for you to do all you can—or at least all you want to do. Make memories for later days. You have earned the rest and the right, and now is your time to bring to life those dreams and desires. Yes, your family still has your attention, but you are seasoned enough to recognize that it's time to nurture yourself, to give birth to the sleeping visions that you've carried for so long.

Adding to your delight: while you are giving birth to your visions, you are reaping the rewards of a life molded by the hand of the Master. You are experiencing the richness of being among His blessed and highly favored. Because you've been in His care and under His supervision, you are beginning to glean the harvest from seeds planted during your younger days. This is a marvelous time for you. Somewhere in the back of your mind and in between the scraggly lines of life, you know God has saved the best for last for you.

WRINKLES: TROPHIES IN THE TRASH

Just as God hides treasures about Himself in the darkness—in the fiery trials we pass through—He also hides you and me, His handiwork and His trophies, in unexpected places. It is not reasonable to expect to find fine china sitting on the bed of a dump truck; nor do we anticipate finding baskets of pearls discarded alongside the highway. But we must have a keen eye to see what God has placed amongst us. He hid Jesus in a barn; He concealed the birth of the King of Glory in an obscure and unusual place. It was His design that placed flowers amongst the thorns and rubies amidst rubble.

We cannot use the eyeglass of the world to see the priceless treasures and trophies God has placed around us. Wrinkles, for example, are something we see as ugly signs of age. But what do wrinkles represent? If they are hallmarks of our endurance, they cannot blur our beauty.

We cannot look for the lights of this world in radiant places, since light is found in darkness; it is more apt to be revealed in the most unlikely environments. For example,

God places His wisdom in the lined face of an old woman with weak knees and failing sight. Within her, you will find volumes of knowledge and understanding. He positions you, His prized possession, in problematic circumstances — but because your condition does not reflect your position in God, you mistakenly begin to doubt that you are in His will or that you have favor with Him. We must trust God when we cannot trace Him and know that His plan for our lives will ultimately have a wonderful and productive outcome.

> **WE MUST TRUST GOD WHEN WE CANNOT TRACE HIM.**

TRASH TO TREASURE

Perhaps you've noticed from time to time, as I have, an old, shabbily dressed woman digging through a trash barrel. Did you notice the delight on her face if she found a partially eaten hamburger or a soda can still containing a soft drink? Were you amazed, as I was, at the exhilaration she expressed to find someone else's leftovers? Can you even understand anyone who is thrilled to discover trash in a garbage can? But the old saying is true: one person's rubbish is another person's treasure.

I sometimes think of how God picked up my squandered, fruitless life and began to put together the scattered scraps of my existence to make something worthwhile, to fashion someone He could use for His purpose.

You may be moving through this world, wandering about, disconnected from rich relationships. You may feel discarded because of your lack of true friends or loving family members. You feel anything but blessed and highly favored. For whatever reason, you may feel as if you are in exile, isolated from nurturing and rewarding associations. As a daughter of God, you may be passing through a season of seclusion.

Regardless of how you came to be alone, however, do not feel lonely, since the God who resides inside of you is closer than anyone else could ever manage to be. That someone threw you away doesn't make you worthless. To God you are priceless.

WOMEN OF EXILE

Some women do not feel their value before God, because society has taught them they are failures or have nothing to offer. These include divorced women, widows, single moms, so-called old maids—you can add to the list. Many, many women who have gone through painful traumas actually feel exiled: undesirable and worthless.

I recently taught a workshop on divorce at our church. It is a hard topic, but one I know well. Still, since I've been divorced now for many years, I was a little shaken by the grief and the low self-esteem that greeted me when I began speaking. I looked out at the sad faces of men and women and began to remember my own low state all those years ago.

I believe God hates divorce. But I don't believe He hates the people who divorce. I believe He hates the anger, bitterness, strife, and anxiety that result from divorce. I believe He hates the pain and harm that it causes His children. Often, divorce leaves people so injured and humiliated that they feel they are of no value. But God who heals diseases also heals broken hearts. In fact, He came especially for the wounded. Jesus said,

> The Spirit of the Lord is upon me, because he hath anointed me to preach the gospel to the poor; he hath sent me to heal the brokenhearted, to preach deliverance to the captives, and recovering of sight to the blind, to set at liberty them that are bruised, to preach the acceptable year of the Lord.
>
> (Luke 4:18–19 KJV)

If you are God's woman and have experienced any kind of loss or ostracism, no longer see yourself as unworthy or unwanted. You've learned much about relationships, and as time passes and healing occurs, you'll help and encourage someone else who has to walk this same pathway. Wrinkles earned from your hard times will not blemish your beauty— they will only enhance it.

WRINKLES EARNED FROM YOUR HARD TIMES WILL NOT BLEMISH YOUR BEAUTY—THEY WILL ONLY ENHANCE IT.

Perhaps, though, you need relief from your pain and struggle today. If so, this is a season to walk closely with God so that He may carefully guide you through the emotional upheaval you are experiencing. I can assure you that He will get you safely through this period, and your future will be bright and refreshing.

Go on with your life and your living, and let God heal you until you no longer suffer. Be healed in your heart so that you are free to love again. Be healed so completely that you can unwrap the bloody bandages of another soul. Let God's love flow through you until you are made tender again.

BLEMISHES: THE POLLUTION OF THE WORLD

Trophy Woman, don't waste your wilderness experience. It's important that we maintain our deliverance once God has redeemed us from our circumstances.

The Scriptures tell us to keep unspotted from evil influences: "Religion that God our Father accepts as pure and faultless is this: to look after orphans and widows in their distress and to keep oneself from being polluted by the world" (James 1:27).

Yes, that means to keep morally unblemished, but there are other ways to become soiled. We want to beware of those people, places, and things that do not support our higher call in Christ. Whom and what you expose yourself to is just as important as how you view life and what you do with it.

As a child, I often heard Momma repeat this well-known axiom: "Association brings on assimilation." You don't want to forfeit any of what you've learned by constant interaction with people who do not share your vision or possess your understanding. It is critical that we feed our minds and nurture our spirits with life.

You and I are aware that not all women of God enjoy the same level of understanding or have the same aspirations and goals in Christ. The Bible describes such people as "silly":

> For wrath killeth the foolish man, and envy slayeth the silly one. (Job 5:2 KJV)

> They . . . creep into houses, and lead captive silly women laden with sins, led away with divers lusts, ever learning, and never able to come to the knowledge of the truth. (2 Timothy 3:6–7 KJV)

Look at silly women: Silly women are petty. They are gossips who spend their time monitoring the lives of other people. They are women who compare themselves with others and are envious of what they have yet to obtain. Silly women waste time thinking about things that do not matter. A silly woman would rather hear herself talk than listen to wisdom. This woman can't apply the truths she hears Sunday after Sunday and Bible study after Bible study; she is a broken and leaky vessel that must be patched again and again. Silly women are not in tune with God.

> SILLY WOMEN ARE NOT IN TUNE WITH GOD.

Most of us don't want to be silly women, yet many are led astray by others who have not been refined in the Refiner's fire. I said in the last chapter that when God leads you into the wilderness, into a "valley of the shadow of death" experience, it takes the foolishness and the silliness out of you. I don't want to imply that you won't have fun and enjoy your life, but you will be careful not to squander the character development Christ has wrought in you through your personal struggles. You simply won't allow blemishes to mar your trophy by entertaining vain and unimportant matters.

ARE YOU SILLY OR SHINY?

Once you've been in the Refiner's fire, after you've been melted down through human struggle, you become clearheaded, keen, and more able to hear God's direction in your life. When fine vessels are made, the artist uses abrasives to rub out blemishes and sharp instruments to bring out detail. What tools and gadgets is God using to etch His design onto the landscape of your life—the surface of your trophy? More than anything, God wants to bring out the best in each of us, and He allows carefully monitored events and circumstances to produce the results He seeks to see in you and me.

He uses our experiences to bring us to low places that we might seek His face: "People brought all their sick to him

and begged him to let the sick just touch the edge of his cloak, and all who touched him were healed" (Matt. 14:35–36).

God wants our attention, our wholeness, and most assuredly He wants relationship with us. God is maturing His women so that we may have fellowship with Him, our Father and our Creator. In order to reign and rule with Him, we must first undergo a significant process so that we are made credible and qualified, whole and complete.

GOD WANTS OUR ATTENTION, OUR WHOLENESS, AND MOST ASSUREDLY HE WANTS RELATIONSHIP WITH US.

Sister, you just are not really real until you have a real encounter with God. That kind of encounter almost always happens through tough times. I've mentioned that generally, people do not seek God's face until life has turned upside down on them. Very few people seek Him until it is the time of trouble. When troubles come, fight the spiritual blemishes; shine as a trophy.

THE MARKS OF LOVE

When I think of God's molding and making in our lives, I am reminded of the children's story *The Velveteen Rabbit*. You know it: A little boy has a room filled with toys. Among them is a very old Skin Horse and a new Velveteen Rabbit. One day the plush rabbit asks the ragged Skin Horse what is "real." The horse replies that real is when you are loved and cared for and nurtured: held until your fur begins to rub off and your hair begins to shed and your joints begin to come out of place. It is at this stage that you become real.

When you begin to possess that raggedy look, it is the look of love. To the untrained eye, you'll look tattered and torn. You may not appear desirable. But to the wise, you'll have an aura about you that says, "I've mattered to Someone. I am special to God."

Look into the eyes of a woman who has walked steadily with God. Her wisdom, her understanding, and her strength are soothing. She is an encouragement to others. She has survived, and her ability to thrive through turbulent times makes us want to shout to God with joy. The results of walking with God are always evident and tremendous and admirable.

> THE RESULTS OF WALKING WITH GOD ARE ALWAYS
> EVIDENT AND TREMENDOUS AND ADMIRABLE.

Perhaps you are recovering from a deep loss. Know this: behind all of God's Trophy Women are powerful testimonies of God's strong hand sustaining and shaping their lives. You are the evidence, the living proof, that despite life-threatening circumstances, you can cross a personal Red Sea by the miracle-working power of your God.

What makes you so precious to God is your personal experience with Him. What you know about God from your

seasons of testing makes you wise, and wisdom makes you powerful. Once you've tasted the goodness and mercies of God, once you've experienced the strength that rescues you and the voice that soothes you, you'll be like the woman in the Song of Solomon: always chasing after your Beloved. Always wanting to be in His presence. Always longing to be near Him.

Remember not to measure your life with the world's tape measure. Yes, you lost that position and now you make a fraction of your previous income. Yes, you are in the midst of raising a seemingly incorrigible child. Yes, a once-precious relationship is slipping like sand through your fingers. But you cannot let sad situations make you ashamed of who you are in Christ. What the enemy means for evil, God will make good. Just as Joseph declared, "You intended to harm me, but God intended it for good" (Gen. 50:20).

Trophy Woman in-the-making, what may be a disappointing and discouraging experience today is only preparation for a radiant and promising future. You know that if you had never had any problems, you would never see the mercy of God solve them.

Your life may look a mess right now; your current lifestyle may not mirror your beliefs or your destiny. You might even feel utterly without value. Do not be discouraged. Instead, remember the bag lady, see her smile, hear her sigh of relief, and recall her delight in finding priceless treasures and trophies everywhere, even in the trash. If you look closely enough, you'll find some too.

God's Trophy Women

I celebrate you
For rising from the
Ashes of your past,
The sorrow of your situation and
The barriers set against you.

I celebrate you for the
Battles you've won, accompanied
By your kind and generous heart.
I celebrate your calm, cool resolve
And your hard-earned spirit of wisdom.

I celebrate your
Dreams, your vision and your future,
Your fortitude and your destiny.

I celebrate your soft femininity and fierce faith.
I celebrate your good works and your great mind.

God's Trophy Women destined for
Greatness, made great
Shine Bright!

Questions for Reflection

❦ *Have you allowed perceived imperfections to drive you to obsessive correction? What was or is the result?*

❦ *Whatever your age, how do you view the "dusk" of life? What do you—or will you—have to offer in those years to others?*

❦ *When Jacqueline's grandmother found that life wouldn't bend for her, she bent for it. In what ways can you "bend" for life today, rather than fighting inevitable change?*

❦ *When have you seen "flowers amongst the thorns"? If you haven't, how can you begin to do so?*

❦ *Are you "real"? What "marks of love" do you bear today because you have been truly loved?*

Prayer

Father,

I thank You and praise You for Your Son, Jesus. Thank You for bringing light into this dark world. Thank You for my sister, who is precious in Your sight.

Lord, bless this woman today to realize and appropriate the beaming presence of God. Let her feel built up in You, God. This woman is valuable to heaven; let her sense her worth and Your approval of her life.

Give her, Father God, the faith, the aspiration, and the confidence to be all that You've made her to be. Let her feel the support and approval of Your love that she might be strong in You and a vessel of blessings to others. Lift her today with Your love, Your light, and Your Word. Guide her through this world, secure in Your arms and in Your peace.

Thank You, Father, for letting her see the gleam in Your eye, special to her.

In Jesus' name, amen.

8

FINISHING TOUCHES

Life is at work in you.

It's been said that Jesus did more than anyone on the face of the globe to make better the lives of women. When I first heard this, I was too young, chronologically and spiritually, to understand. Today I am more aware of the atrocities that women have endured since their entrance on this planet.

Misogyny is not a new subject. The hatred of women has existed since early human history. For centuries, countless women have been oppressed and treated like property. We know the crimes against women are appalling. Female subjugation worldwide is shocking to our Western mind-set. Gender discrimination is illegal in this country, yet in many places it is thriving. Women only recently received the right to vote in the United States (1920 is our recent past!).

Many women continue to reside in a place of despair just because they are female. If you are one of those women, I challenge you to believe that God is mindful of where you are and that your substandard place is man-made. Why do I believe this? Because I know that prayer changes things.

Many years ago, while struggling, underemployed, sickly, and oftentimes frightened, I struggled to walk by faith and not by sight. Isn't that exactly the right thing to do? We must pray and believe God, no matter what we see with our natural eyes. Looking through the eyes of the Spirit, we must see a bright future for ourselves. It took me a long time to come out of that dark place, but I did come out. And you can too.

If you ever feel you are "less than" as a female, know that God sees you quite differently. I'll explain more about this in the pages ahead.

WOMEN: CLEANSED BY THE BLOOD

America's first African-American congresswoman, the late Shirley Chisholm, an outspoken advocate for women and minorities, has been quoted as saying, "Of my two handicaps, being female put more obstacles in my path than being black." These are words from the twentieth century. We can only imagine life for women during the ministry of Jesus Christ.

> "BEING FEMALE PUT MORE OBSTACLES IN MY PATH THAN BEING BLACK." —SHIRLEY CHISHOLM

Many writings reveal that the traditions and customs of that day regarded women as inferior. Women were basically "owned" by their fathers, their brothers, and their husbands. Long before Jesus came, Moses had instituted laws for sanitation and hygiene that were translated into the idea that women were vessels filled with impurities. Now, the Law itself was not misogynistic, but man's interpretation perverted the Law.

> When a woman has her regular flow of blood, the impurity of her monthly period will last seven days, and anyone who touches her will be unclean till evening. Anything she lies on will be unclean, and anything she sits on will be unclean. Whoever touches her bed must wash his clothes and bathe with water, and he will be unclean till evening. (Leviticus 15:19–21)

> A woman who becomes pregnant and gives birth to a son will be ceremonially unclean for seven days, just as she is unclean during her monthly period. . . . Then the woman must wait thirty-three days to be purified from her bleeding. She must not touch anything sacred or go to the sanctuary until the days of her purification are over. (Leviticus 12:2–4)

These laws were still in place when Christ was born. Luke 2:22 tells us that even Mary had to abide by the laws after the birth of Jesus: "When the time of their purification according

to the Law of Moses had been completed, Joseph and Mary took [Jesus] to Jerusalem to present him to the Lord."

So for centuries, women were considered "unclean" and were therefore not allowed the same privileges as men. This attitude pervaded more than simple guidelines for hygiene. In fact, before Jesus descended on the scene, women moved through a male-dominated society. Simply because one was born woman, she was denied the respect and the human freedoms she deserved.

It is critical that every born-again, believing woman not see herself as unclean or inferior. Our Bible clearly tells us that what God has cleansed is forever purified: "We have been made holy through the sacrifice of the body of Jesus Christ once for all" (Heb. 10:10). Woman of God, you are clean enough! (If you struggle with feeling forgiven, see the prayer at the end of this chapter.)

> IT IS CRITICAL THAT EVERY BORN-AGAIN, BELIEVING WOMAN NOT SEE HERSELF AS UNCLEAN OR INFERIOR.

JESUS CHANGES EVERYTHING

Life before the death, burial, and resurrection of Jesus was completely different from what most women experience today. At the time of Jesus' ministry, men perceived women as the reason for their immoral behavior and treated them as inferiors. Women's fathers arranged their marriages.

Rabbis did not teach women. Women could not enter the holy places within the temple. During this period of time, men did not acknowledge women in public. Men did not talk with women, not even their wives, unless they were in a private place. Can you fathom the miserable mental and emotional conditions of these first-century females?

I find it fascinating that when Jesus arrived, everything began to change for women. Jesus disrupted the order of all things: throughout His ministry, He esteemed and included women. Jesus' revolutionary contact with women began showing a better way to treat females. During His day-to-day ministry, Jesus revealed the heart of God toward His female creation. Like dawn breaking in on the dark, He began to peel back the layers of ignorance and to transform the thinking and traditions of His people.

Jesus began to reveal just how much women mattered to Him. He revealed women's worth not through His preaching but through His actions. In open display, on numerous occasions in the Scripture, He allows us to see His belief about gender. The Jesus we witness in the New Testament is quite clear about the value of a woman.

> THE JESUS WE WITNESS IN THE NEW TESTAMENT IS
> QUITE CLEAR ABOUT THE VALUE OF A WOMAN.

Through the Scriptures, we see Jesus breaking curses and delivering women into virtuous and honorable positions. His responses to women affect our relationship with

Him today. Clearly, His message to women communicated redemption and liberation.

JESUS SPEAKS TO WOMEN

Although tradition clearly did not allow public conversations between men and women, we see Jesus breaking this tradition early on: John 4 says,

> Jesus, tired as he was from the journey, sat down by the well. . . . When a Samaritan woman came to draw water, Jesus said to her, "Will you give me a drink?" The Samaritan woman said to him, "You are a Jew and I am a Samaritan woman. How can you ask me for a drink?" (For Jews do not associate with Samaritans.) Jesus answered her, "If you knew the gift of God and who it is that asks you for a drink, you would have asked him and he would have given you living water." (vv. 6–10)

This woman, shunned both for her sex and for her ethnicity, was one Jesus engaged in conversation about spiritual matters. He did not treat her as untouchable or unworthy.

Time after time, we see Jesus touching and talking and ministering to the women of His day.

JESUS HEALS WOMEN

Although men in Jesus' day considered women nothing more than property, Jesus saw their human pain.

On a Sabbath Jesus was teaching in one of the synagogues, and a woman was there who had been crippled by a spirit for eighteen years. She was bent over and could not straighten up at all. When Jesus saw her, he called her forward and said to her, "Woman, you are set free from your infirmity." Then he put his hands on her, and immediately she straightened up and praised God. (Luke 13:10–13)

Jews were to perform no work on the Sabbath. What Jesus did was unlawful (according to Pharisee standards) and completely shocking. Because women were ignored or invisible prior to His coming to the earth, His extreme behavior toward them drew their hearts to gladly follow in His ministry.

Jesus didn't see women as other men did. To Him, they were not offensive or embarrassing. He saw their isolation and their critical situations. He saw their hearts and their total need for His salvation. And He saw their importance and usefulness to God.

Jesus Responds to Broken Hearts

Look at the widow of Nain burying her only son. In that instance, Jesus again acted against the Jewish customs and laws and did the unthinkable: He touched a coffin, an "unclean" act. Witness His tenderness in this scene:

Jesus went to a town called Nain, and his disciples and a large crowd went along with him. As he

approached the town gate, a dead person was being carried out—the only son of his mother, and she was a widow. And a large crowd from the town was with her. When the Lord saw her, his heart went out to her and he said, "Don't cry." Then he went up and touched the coffin, and those carrying it stood still. He said, "Young man, I say to you, get up!" The dead man sat up and began to talk, and Jesus gave him back to his mother. (Luke 7:11–15)

Jesus cared intensely about the sufferings of women, and He took action to alleviate the discomfort and disorder of their lives. Many times, the Bible says that women fell at His feet worshiping. We can see why. When you are in the presence of an astonishing, wonder-working Person who cares about you and your gender, you are humbled and overwhelmed.

JESUS HONORS WOMEN

Jesus was a revolutionary. In a time when men ignored women, Jesus esteemed them and called for their humane treatment. Look at Mark 14:3–6:

While he was in Bethany, reclining at the table in the home of a man known as Simon the Leper, a woman came with an alabaster jar of very expensive perfume, made of pure nard. She broke the jar and poured the perfume on his head.

Some of those present were saying indignantly to one another, "Why this waste of perfume? It could have been sold for more than a year's wages and the money given to the poor." And they rebuked her harshly.

"Leave her alone," said Jesus. "Why are you bothering her? She has done a beautiful thing to me."

Jesus took the men to task for hassling this woman. Look at Him coming to her aid. It was virtually unheard of for women to receive this kind of support.

Jesus' care and concern have not changed. He is the same today.

How many times have you been in a situation where someone or some circumstance has vexed your spirit? Can you now hear Him saying, "Why are you bothering her?" He is emphatically saying, "Leave her alone! Why would you harass her? Stop needling this woman." We need more men and women to take His stance and to see things Jesus' way.

Public Problem, Public Deliverance

Ladies, Jesus is our Superhero, our Superman, and our Knight in shining armor. He is the one who rescues us from fields of trouble. Once the Maker has performed the alterations necessary to our character and disposition, He moves more profoundly into the role of caretaker and begins to put finishing touches on us, His trophies, His women whom He blesses and highly favors.

> ## JESUS IS OUR SUPERHERO, OUR SUPERMAN,
> ## AND OUR KNIGHT IN SHINING ARMOR.

He often does this in a public display. For example, have you ever had a problem many others knew about, and God openly resolved it so that others saw you had His favor and attention? Maybe you struggled to provide for your family, and everyone saw you were going through tough times. Perhaps it was obvious that your marriage was on the rocks. Or maybe you've battled an illness for a long time.

Women cannot always hide their problems. Sometimes our trouble is on display. But look at how Jesus dealt with so many women's issues publicly to show His approval and endorsement of them—not of their situations, but of their personhood. He valued those women as individuals. Isn't He doing the same today with you and me?

I believe God allows us sometimes to have public humiliations and struggles so we might be examples of His deliverance. He certainly makes better vessels of us from our calamities. Remember, we are "living epistles read of men" (see 2 Cor. 3:2–3) and more often than not, our lives are orchestrated that God might get the glory.

One of my favorite Scriptures is in the Psalms. I found it during the darkest period of my recovery. Strangely, it is not a traditional healing Scripture. Or, at least initially, it didn't appear to be a passage known for comforting the sick: "By this I know that thou favourest me, because mine enemy doth not triumph over me" (41:11 KJV).

For each and every battle God has brought me through, my faith has grown stronger. I know beyond a shadow of a doubt that God has been favoring me. My enemy has not triumphed over me. What about you? What has occurred or is taking place now over which you are habitually triumphant? Maybe you haven't received total victory, but the fact that God keeps making a way out of no way is reason to rejoice.

> THE FACT THAT GOD KEEPS MAKING A WAY
> OUT OF NO WAY IS REASON TO REJOICE.

Today, God is saying to the enemy of your soul, "Why are you bothering her? Leave her alone. Back up. Nothing you do to her will ever prosper because I am for her, and that is more than the world against her." If you pause a moment to recognize that each triumph, no matter how minute, is still a victory and God's way of redirecting trouble away from you, you will begin to grow stronger with each revelation of His favor and mercy unto you.

As our generation of women begins to feel the pulse of God's heart and to walk in the love God has for us, His affirmation is sure to be revelatory in a way that changes the life and the status of each woman of God. Seeing that He is so mindful of us, we are endeared to Him all the more.

NOT EVEN AN HONORABLE MENTION

I love the Lord for many reasons. One is because He is so fair—He is an equalizer. He is a Savior to the uttermost and

He abides sweetly inside the secret sanctuary of our souls. When He performs His work of redemption, He leaves nothing out. Over time, He changes our lives, our perceptions, our attitudes, and even our characters. He makes what was unseemly and inappropriate, fit. The Scriptures declare that He makes all things beautiful in His time.

I think it is important for me to reveal four women buried in the genealogies of the Bible. In Matthew 1, we find a long list of Jesus' forebears. But have you ever noticed the female thread that runs through this tapestry?

What is so unusual about this unassuming passage of Scripture is the omission of the names of women who *could have* been listed in the lineage of Christ, such as Sarah, Rebekah, and Rachel. But their names are, in fact, missing from the text.

Sarah, who is listed in the Hall of Faith (Heb. 11) for her belief; Sarah, who believed God and birthed Isaac in her old age, is not mentioned. You know Sarah. You could write a book on all of her wonderful, admirable qualities. Yet Sarah is not named in the lineage of Christ.

And there's no mention of Rachel. You remember her too. Rachel was ever so lovely. This woman looked so good that her husband worked seven years for her hand in marriage. And when he was tricked into working an additional seven to marry her, he did it. Fourteen years of hard labor to marry this woman—she must have been stunning. Yet Rachel is not listed in the lineage of Christ.

Rebekah's name doesn't appear in this passage of

Matthew either. Rebekah, the woman of God who represents fine qualities, service, and character, receives no recognition. Do you remember that when Isaac's servant came for water, she not only gave him water but all of his camels as well (Gen. 24)? Sounds like hard work to me, but Rebekah was a woman of high standards and workmanship. Yet like the others, she is missing from the distinguished lineup leading to the birth of Christ. She didn't even receive an honorable mention!

MEET FOUR TROPHY WOMEN: TAMAR, RAHAB, BATHSHEBA, AND RUTH

Now imagine with me that you were biologically related to Christ. You would have a ledger, multiple copies of birth certificates, a finely mapped family tree, affidavits, documentaries, and every piece of evidence possible to show that you belonged in the group. You know how some folks act when they are related to someone famous. At the least, you would expect to find your name among the others in such a prestigious lineage.

But look at this passage of Scripture and notice whom God reveals to be in the family. Look at the women to whom He gives such notoriety:

A record of the genealogy of Jesus Christ the son of David, the son of Abraham: Abraham was the father of Isaac, Isaac the father of Jacob, Jacob the father of Judah and his brothers, Judah the father of Perez and Zerah, whose mother was Tamar . . . Salmon the father

of Boza, whose mother was Rahab, Boaz the father of Obed, whose mother was Ruth, Obed the father of Jesse, and Jesse the father of King David. David was the father of Solomon, whose mother had been Uriah's wife [Bathsheba]. (vv. 1–3, 4–6)

First we find, buried in the "begats" of Matthew 1, *Tamar*. I heard you gasp. Why did God give this woman a place of recognition?

Tamar was the woman who dressed up as a prostitute, played the harlot to sleep with none other than her father-in-law, Judah. You read that right. It is one of several shocking stories in the Bible (Gen. 38:11–26). She was a childless and desperate woman, perhaps trying to continue the family lineage, who went to extreme measures. By taking matters into her own hands, she devised an immoral scheme. Who can understand her behavior? Only God. He still lists Tamar in the impressive lineup leading to the birth of the Son of God.

What is God saying to us by giving this woman such an honorable mention? Surely we recognize the compassion of God toward her. Long after Tamar has passed off the scene, He is saying that she mattered, that she was a woman of worth, and that He is not ashamed of her past. The desperate actions of Tamar's life did not destroy her destiny to become one among the "greats" in Christ's lineage.

Tamar experienced firsthand the severity of life's fires, yet God's mercy made her shine throughout history. She is a Trophy Woman.

So many of you reading this book have a past. Many women, through no fault of their own, have suffered at the hands of unrighteous men and women. God sees that, and He opens the door of the church and of His heart to you. You are not locked out of His love, or His embrace. Upon acceptance of His invitation, Trophy-Woman-in-the-making, you come to a place where He can wash your remembrance and restore you from the inside out. He removes the slag and the impurities from your life so that you may evolve into a stunning masterpiece. Nothing in your past, present, or future can stop Him from accomplishing His purpose in Your life.

Who else receives His special attention in Matthew? I know you can hardly believe it, but yes, there's Rahab's name. You remember Rahab, the harlot (Josh. 2, 6). I wonder why God didn't keep her a secret? Why didn't He simply omit the name of this scarlet woman? Because He calls to women like Rahab. He uses and delivers such women; he molds and buffs such women till they are trophies. I know of women who have practiced the oldest profession in the world, but today they are serving God with all of their hearts. There is nothing too hard for God. They've become Trophy Women through the shed blood of Jesus and through their testimony of His grace and mercy.

Even Uriah's wife, Bathsheba, is not excluded from the grace of God (2 Sam. 11–12). Despite her adultery, her name also appears in the exclusive list of Christ's predecessors. Am I supporting sin? Of course not! I want to emphasize to women with a past: if you've confessed your sin to the

Father, believe God for His forgiveness. You are no different from any other person. God is a purifier. What God calls clean is clean. Whom God designates as a Trophy Woman *is*, by His power, one of His shining masterpieces.

You, my sister, may be the uncelebrated woman with a past and the least likely to be recognized, but God has written your name in the palm of His hand (Isa. 49:16). What an honorable mention!

Then we see Ruth the Moabitess, an outsider, initially an unbeliever, included in the lineage of Christ (the book of Ruth). God can accept anyone into His church. God can take anyone's life and add the polish that makes a trophy.

You know how some people are today: "If you don't look like me, you can't fellowship with me." Some women are excluded because they are "different." But God sends us a loud and clear message that all are welcome into His body, His family. The only requirement is that you are a believer in the Lord Jesus Christ. The church is an ethnicity in its own right, and we are a diverse people by God's design and planning.

Ruth was a woman once outside God's family. Yet when death took her husband prematurely, she abandoned her homeland in order to follow and serve her mother-in-law, Naomi, and Naomi's God. Ruth endured the sudden death of her husband, a traumatic move to a new city and people, and her mother-in-law's relentless bitterness about how life had turned out. Because Ruth persisted through the pain, she became a Trophy Woman.

What I want you to see is that you and other believers in the Lord Jesus Christ are not locked out of heaven's curio by what you did yesterday in secret places or because of your race. The woman the Lord sets free is free indeed. When the trophies are lined up for showcasing, no one looks at one and says, "Well, this one had more impurities than the other." No. All anyone sees are beautiful, finished products. It really doesn't so much matter how you start—it matters how you finish.

JESUS CALLS WOMEN TO HIS CHURCH, TO BE THE CHURCH

Christ ushers women to a high platform, because the kingdom needs the expression of women. It needs the woman's touch. Women manifest God in a myriad of soft and tender ways. He has need of our marked and marvelous differences, and we have need of Him.

Jesus has come to take what has been called unclean and to call it clean. He has come to the unworthy, the despised, and the undesirable to give His approval. He has come to the unloved and the despicable. He has come for those others don't want. Among that group, we find women.

Every woman of God should rejoice in the God of her salvation: Jesus. He came to make men *and* women free. We women should be the first to thank God for Jesus. Boldly, He recognized and honored women during a time when others overlooked or ostracized them. Jesus elevates women

to let others know that females matter to God as much as men do.

When the woman with the "issue of blood" (Mark 5:25 KJV) touched the hem of His clothing, this was an outlandish act. In fact, this woman, in her condition, was forbidden to leave her dwelling. Physical contact with anyone was also forbidden. Of course, Jesus knew all of this, but none of it stopped Him from bringing her to the forefront by asking, "Who touched me?" He shined the spotlight on this woman to draw attention to God's compassion for all of His people, men and women alike. He applauded her, noting that her faith had made her well.

Hooray for Jesus! There is none like Him! Today, He is still touching, healing, acknowledging, and applauding women. And for that, we should be eternally grateful.

Every woman wants to encounter an earthly man with Jesus' attributes. Certainly every Christian single woman praying to God for a husband ought pray to God for a man like Jesus. (See the poem at the end of this chapter!)

> TODAY, HE IS STILL TOUCHING, HEALING, ACKNOWLEDGING, AND APPLAUDING WOMEN.

Doesn't it make your heart rejoice to know that you are special to God? Aren't you delighted to know that the Creator of the universe, the CEO of the planet, thinks you are wonderful? God has bestowed His grace and His attention upon the ones who were once called unclean. He has made His face to shine upon His women. Aren't you glad? Don't you love Him for loving you?

The woman with the alabaster jar certainly did. There was a woman who was grateful. There was a woman who had been made free. There was a woman who wasted lavishly a year's salary—the cost of the precious ointment—on Jesus to say to Him: "I adore You for seeing me, for recognizing me, and for making me whole. I adore You for your bodacious and unapologetic message to the world that I matter." She worshiped Him because He was the Savior of her soul, and she worshiped Him because He was her Hero.

WOMEN RESPOND TO JESUS

In Luke 10:42, Jesus told Martha that her sister, Mary, who was sitting at His feet listening to His words, had "chosen what is better." Jesus openly invites women to partake of His ministry, His teachings, and His direction. Yes, Martha, who was serving, was doing right to prepare the food and serve the visitors, but Mary did better to avail herself of the life-giving words of Jesus Christ. Mary had stepped into the liberating presence of the Master.

Can you see how exceptional and precious you are to God? Will you ever read the Gospels again without seeing how special God thinks you are? Did you realize how good God is to His women? Feel the frenzy of the women following Jesus! These women had found their Emancipator. They had found the Lover of their souls, and they were

doing anything to support Him in His work on this earth. Luke 8:3 says, "Joanna the wife of Cuza, the manager of Herod's household; Susanna; and many others . . . were helping to support them [Jesus and the disciples] out of their own means."

Clearly, Jesus had struck a nerve with the women of His day. His message was so inclusive of females that it shook them to their cores. Even Pilate's wife was affected. When Pilate was deliberating over whom to send to crucifixion, his wife sent him a note: "Don't have anything to do with that innocent man, for I have suffered a great deal today in a dream because of him" (Matt. 27:19). Why was she so concerned about what happened to Jesus? Is it possible that she too was flabbergasted at the way this man treated women?

In fact, Jesus' kindness moved women to zealously follow Him. This is apparent when we read of his being led to the cross: "A large number of people followed him, including women who mourned and wailed for him" (Luke 23:27). Women, in fact, followed Him all the way to Golgotha and beyond to the Resurrection.

You can imagine why. If someone befriends you, loves you, and treats you as a person of worth and integrity—particularly if that has never or only rarely happened before—how would you feel? For the first time in your life, you realize you count and that someone cares for you uniquely and truthfully. The women of the Bible were overwhelmed, and we should be too.

It was the women who were present after Christ rose from the grave. Luke 24:1 tells us that on the Friday after Jesus' death, "women took the spices they had prepared [to prepare His body for burial] and went to the tomb"— where they encountered two mystical beings who announced Jesus' resurrection. The women He had healed from sickness and from demonic spirits, the women He had cleansed and set free, remained with Him to the end. After His resurrection, Jesus appeared to Mary Magdalene first, sending her to tell the others that He had risen from the grave (John 20:10–18). Perhaps He appeared to a woman first because He knew she would rejoice to see His return, in a way and for reasons others could not.

And today it is no different! Jesus embraces us as we become a part of His church. Jesus always comes to those who look for Him. The Scriptures tell us that Jesus will return to earth for those "who have longed for his appearing" (2 Tim. 4:8), and again, women will rejoice to see Him.

One of Jesus' greatest acts, but one of the least mentioned, is His forming relationships with women. Jesus is the one who set women free. He is the one who ushered the women into a place of prominence—a place they had never before experienced. He does the same today, through His love, acknowledgment, and appreciation of us. Do you, as one of God's Trophy Women, now understand God's partiality toward you? He chose to love you. He came for the despised, the outcast, the lowly. He came for you and me.

ONE OF JESUS' GREATEST ACTS IS HIS FORMING
RELATIONSHIPS WITH WOMEN.

Daughters of the Most High God, know that you are precious in His sight. You, His trophies, must always thank God for Jesus. He has shown us our importance and our special place with the Father. No matter what your circumstances, always acknowledge the value of your femininity to Christ. It is important that we women understand our position as women who believe in the Lord. We have clout with God simply because we are His women—His Trophy Women.

If I Had a Man Like You

If I had a Man like You
I could wrap my soul around Your essence
Like ivy climbs a tree.
If I had a Man like You I could
Dance in the dark and smile
In the rain.
A Man like You
Spreads hot coals on cold wind chills
And makes life
Tranquil and enchanting.
A Man like You could
Take the shriek out of my
Life and leave me renewed and
Filled with peace.
New like morning dew
Any woman could be devoted
To a Man like You.
A Man like You would forever
Be my treasure chest
Set ablaze with my love.
Oh God, I wish I had a Man like You!

 *Questions for Reflection*

❦ *Has being a woman ever placed obstacles in your path? Why? How did you handle the situation(s)?*

❦ *Do you think God sees you as an inferior being? What evidence do you have for your belief?*

❦ *Which of the stories of Jesus and women is your favorite? Why? How do you relate to it?*

❦ *Aside from providing your salvation, has Jesus ever been a hero to you? When and how?*

❦ *Why do you think Jesus appeared first to a woman after His resurrection?*

Prayer

Great God,

We thank You and adore You for Your kindnesses to Your daughters. Bless Your name for Your way of thinking about women. Lord, we can't thank You enough for how good You've been to each of us. We exalt Your name, for You have filled our mouths with praise and overwhelmed our hearts with Your goodness.

Thank You, God, for giving us Jesus, and thank You, God, for turning our sadness and our struggles into victories. Because of Your love and concern, we are free to be who You've designed us to be. We are free to do great and mighty exploits in Your name.

Thank You, Father, for believing in your daughters and for seeing us as precious and valuable. You have counted us as prizes and made us worthy in Your sight. You've written our names in the Lamb's book of Life. We will forever give Your name the glory, the honor, and the praise.

In Jesus' name, amen.

9

WELL-KEPT WOMEN: GOD'S SHOWPIECES

Hope does not disappoint us.

ROMANS 5:5

*H*ope for the believing woman is hidden glory. Once you learn its power and importance, you'll be more apt to keep hope alive. Such a woman is a *well-kept woman,* one whom God has sustained through rich and varied trials. A well-kept woman is, of course, a Trophy Woman!

I've spent a lot of time in this book showing you the faces and feelings of great women. Remember, you do not have to be a household name to be a lady of deep faith, a trophy. Great in the eyes of God are the women of faith who walk hand in hand with Him through this world. They have all suffered something to be refined in the Refiner's fire.

Trophy Women are not lacy, lightweight people. Many of them are warriors. My mother was such a woman.

MEET A TROPHY WOMAN: MRS. ODITH P. JAKES

My mother was the youngest of fifteen children. Her family also took in a relative's eight children. Momma told us stories about how she and her siblings and cousins, because there were so few beds, had to sleep head-to-foot. More often than not, she awoke with someone's foot in her mouth! Can you imagine living with that many people?

Then there was food. By the time the adults, visitors, and other children were fed, my mother had little to eat. Although her parents were wonderful, loving, and Bible-believing people, they just didn't have enough to go around for such a large family: not enough beds, food, money, heat. My mother was a child deprived of many of life's necessities.

Do you think she saw her family as dysfunctional? Did she throw a big pity party?

No. She saw herself as a woman well kept by God. Sometimes the things that come against you are the buoy you need to rise from the depths.

Momma chose, in fact, to excel. She graduated from high school at age fifteen, completed four years of college in three, and earned a master's degree. She never ingested the polluted (racist) thinking of those times. She accepted that she didn't live in a perfect world, but that world didn't stop her from creating a good life.

My mother had every reason not to succeed, but she became an educator. She took it upon herself to teach her children how to think correctly, how to perceive life, and how to believe in God. Then she taught others the same values and skills. (A well-kept woman is one who keeps others well too.)

Momma was the strongest, toughest individual I've ever encountered. She was always found serving someone else. She and my father performed community work without hesitancy. I remember when they drove through our neighborhood to pick up people to take them to the voting polls. Many of our neighbors didn't own a car, and my parents knew the importance of getting everyone out to vote. My mother taught us to never give up, to keep hope alive, and to make success a part of our lifestyle.

> MY MOTHER TAUGHT US TO NEVER GIVE UP,
> TO KEEP HOPE ALIVE, AND TO MAKE SUCCESS
> A PART OF OUR LIFESTYLE.

Momma's faith was tried many times, throughout her impoverished childhood and her adult life, especially when my father became ill in the late sixties. Then, people had no centers to go to for kidney dialysis. My mother worked with the doctors and the insurance companies and had a dialysis machine moved to our home, where she herself performed the procedure on my father. Sometimes she heard the machine beeping, signaling that there was a problem, and ran into the room to find blood spilled on the floor.

Before the kidney machine became an option, she drove my father twice a week to a clinic four hours away. She did not take a leave of absence from her job and faithfully reported to work between trips.

Through all of this and more, did my mother fold? No. She was a warrior-woman, one well kept by her God, and she fought the good fight of faith.

Even later, when she had to confront her own illness, she kept her trophy shining.

SOMETIMES THE STRONG AREN'T STRONG ENOUGH

It was only a few years ago that my mother, the most outstanding woman I've ever known, passed away. I believe she was remarkable because incredible parents raised her. Grandpa Richard was quiet and hardworking. Grandma Susie always read her Bible, sat in the "amen corner" of her church, and taught the Scriptures during a time when women were not respected as religious leaders or encouraged to teach and expound upon the gospel. Grandma Susie, another Trophy Woman, was known throughout her community as a servant who made a difference in the lives of others. My mother, then, couldn't help but be exceptional; she had an incredible example.

In spite of that and all of her strength and accomplishments, my mother became ill. Seeing her ill was astonishing because her will was so strong, and I had watched her win so many battles through the years. But as you know, some battles are so severe that no matter how much willpower you have, it is not enough to get you out of harm's way.

My mother was diagnosed with a brain tumor. Ironic, isn't it? First my diagnosis and surgery, then my mother underwent the same surgery. She came through it, but before she could completely recuperate, another surgery was necessary. The tumor was so large, it severely compromised her ventricular system, resulting in a total of six brain surgeries.

At one point, she slipped into a coma. I watched the doctor examine my mother. He took a sharp instrument and dug it, very hard, into the sole of her foot. Momma didn't flinch. He continued with similar tests and she didn't move. The doctors soon began to talk about putting a feeding tube in her. Her mouth was clenched shut and she wasn't responding.

One night, I told my older brother, Ernest, to bring the Walkman and a tape for our next day's visit. When we went into her room, we put the headset on her and adjusted the sound so that she could listen to her younger son, Thomas D. Jakes, preach while she lay sleeping. The moment we turned on the tape, her eyes popped wide open! It was amazing! At the sound of his voice, she awakened. Gradually she began to get well enough for us to fly her back to Dallas.

Although she got a little better, even sitting up and having meals on the veranda and making small talk, her health began again to decline. Alzheimer's reared its ugly head. When she slipped away from this earth, her three children,

her grandchildren, great-grandchild, and friends were around her bed, ushering her into the presence of the Lord.

My mother slipped away like a piece of silk sliding off a shoulder. Soft as a cloud and silent as dew, my mother left her children, the hospital room, and this earth. To some, it may seem that she didn't get the victory or that she wasn't triumphant over her situation, but I don't see it that way. She was greatly loved by her children and others—she was greatly loved and well kept by God—until the end of her life.

I know my mother was one of God's Trophy Women.

TROPHIES ARE MADE FOR CELEBRATION

I distinctly remember the sound of Momma's voice one sunny afternoon. After one surgery and before another, my two brothers and I put her in a wheelchair and rolled her outside onto the balcony of the hospital. The Texas sun was shining brightly. She said, "Oh my, the sun feels so good. It feels so good on me."

My mother lived a full life. She appreciated all God's gifts, even the warmth of the sun. What about you?

I challenge you to notice the small occurrences in your life: the smell of water, the scent of soap, the cleanliness of your space, the warmth of sunlight, the still of night, the sound of music, the smile of a child, and the millions of events that make this life bearable and blessed. These are the things God uses to kiss us in our night seasons. They are sent to caress us, and unless we have a trained eye, a listening ear, and a discerning spirit, we may miss the kiss that comes to comfort our souls.

> UNLESS WE HAVE A DISCERNING SPIRIT, WE MAY MISS THE KISS THAT COMES TO COMFORT OUR SOULS.

You, my sisters, who are now awake and aware and enjoying your life serving the Lord Jesus Christ, choose to celebrate life. Enjoy His blessing and His favor! Celebrate your relationship with Him as you taste His goodness and feel His love flow through your life.

Trophy Woman, after all the adversity you've encountered, and now that God has your full attention, move on into all of His many benefits and blessings. Celebrate the ways He has kept you throughout the storm. You shine, and He wants to reward you.

Watch as He performs mighty deeds for you. Have you noticed that God treats you better than you treat yourself? For example, why do you think He didn't allow your marriage with that man? Why did He allow you to be overlooked for that promotion? Why didn't He let you take that dream cruise? Do you think it was to keep you from fun and pleasure? Of course not! He did it because at this juncture in your life, He refuses to give you anything but His best. You are too precious to do just anything or to attach yourself to just anyone.

THE INTENSE VALUE OF ADVERSITY

When you are one of God's Trophy Women, you have walked through too many trials not to understand how valuable you are to God. I often tell people that God is so good, He'll make up ways to bless you. It is not easy to escape His goodness or to be oblivious to His care. How many times has He kept you from dangerous people and unsafe places? So often, we are mindful of what God has kept us through, but we need to take note of the many things God has prevented from entering our lives.

GOD IS SO GOOD, HE'LL MAKE UP WAYS TO BLESS YOU.

I remember praying for what I thought was a need in my life. I petitioned the Lord so much I was tired of praying the prayer. He didn't give me what I wanted, and ultimately, I had to face the fact that He had said no. Today, I cannot begin to tell you how glad I am for the doors He has closed, for the prayers that He did not agree to, and for the times He did not allow me to have my way. If He had done some of the things I asked, I wouldn't be here to talk with you now, nor would I be the person I am today.

When God allows you to enter and sometimes to remain for a time in a bad situation, I believe it is because He knows He is getting the best from your life. He is revealing, through unusually hard predicaments, the gold and the treasure you possess. By design, He is revealing His finest vessel through unordinary circumstances, through fire.

Someone gave me a tape several years ago. On it, a preacher told the story about a gallant man who had a very apparent physical illness. Yet he was a warrior who went to many battles at the request of his commander. He was known throughout his region for winning impossible skirmishes. His fighting skills were so superior, and he was so brave and fearless, always going to the front line to make war with the enemy, that others feared and respected him.

The man's commander was intensely proud of his abilities and decided to have him cured of his illness. The commander wanted to reward the warrior's fighting victories by removing the physical ailment that was so apparent in his body. The commander decided that if the warrior could win so many battles while ill, he would be even fiercer when his body was restored.

After many doctors were finally able to provide a cure for the warrior, another battle ensued. Amazingly, the commander noticed that his warrior now shrank to the back of the camp. Other skirmishes took place, and the valiant fighter avoided the forefront. He no longer led and won; he hid and lost. He now had something to lose, and he prized it so much that he lost his zeal and his ability to fight and to win. He ultimately became useless to his commander and was released from his duties.

I know that many of you are on God's battlefield, fighting with a limp *but still fighting,* and I believe that this story may shed light on why. Perhaps God knows you are at your best and your highest, not in spite of your adversity, but because of it. This was true even of Jesus: "Though he were a Son, yet learned he obedience by the things which he suffered" (Heb. 5:8 KJV).

> YOU ARE AT YOUR BEST AND YOUR HIGHEST, NOT IN SPITE OF YOUR ADVERSITY, BUT BECAUSE OF IT.

THE ODIOUS WOMAN

Let's look at another kind of woman. In preparing to speak at an event, I came across a surprising Scripture: "For three things the earth is disquieted, and for four which it cannot bear: For a servant when he reigneth; and a fool when he is filled with meat; for an odious woman when she is married; and an handmaid that is heir to her mistress" (Prov. 30:21–23 KJV).

As I began to read this passage, I initially thought that an "odious woman" was one who did not cleanse her body—a woman who carried an offensive odor. But, as I began to examine several translations, to my surprise I discovered that this is really a married woman who is unloved! This is a woman who has not let adversity make her shine. The New International Version states it this way:

> Under three things the earth trembles,
>   under four it cannot bear up:
> a servant who becomes king,

a fool who is full of food,
an unloved woman who is married,
and a maidservant who displaces her mistress.

This woman's distress is such that she disquiets and disrupts the earth. She suffers from such neglect and intense feelings of remorse that her very presence is perplexing to the inhabitants of the earth. Many tremble at her disposition. This woman suffers from lack of appreciation and attention, and she is furious. She has entered into a relationship designed to provide her with nurturing, love, and warmth, but she is not able to receive these things. More than likely, she has spent most of her years clutching her feelings of emptiness while she harbors a lot of stored-up pain. Her insecurity is not cured by marriage but spills over into marriage. Or this is a woman who is married but unloved; she has become bitter because of her husband's rejection and neglect. Either way, the odious woman is one who is unhappy and who does not want others to be blessed.

I strongly caution women to flee from her acidic advice and to pray for her sour attitude. Although she is married, she is unhappy and unkind. She is a male-basher and has nothing good to say about life. Her unkind remarks and insinuations are contagious, and therefore destructive. Her advice to you is always to see about yourself first, to the neglect of your children, your husband, and the other important people in your life.

The odious woman does not believe any love relationships

work out well, and she is a prime example of misery loving company. Her toxic emotions misguide her. This woman's attitude is lethal! Pray for her, but watch as well as pray!

Why do I mention this woman to you? I want to remind you that we are all works in progress. Some are closer to God's highest design than others. I also write to remind you that as God performs mighty works in your life and as the years pass, don't let anything or anyone disrupt your healing relationship with the Lord Jesus Christ. You've been through too much. You've suffered too long to let anyone kill your joy and steal your peace—and tarnish your trophy.

> DON'T LET ANYTHING OR ANYONE DISRUPT YOUR
> HEALING RELATIONSHIP WITH THE LORD JESUS CHRIST.

No longer does anyone have to feel or act like the odious woman. A well-kept woman certainly never will!

TRUST IS WHAT WE COME TO

I've now learned that it is so much easier to let go and let God take over. I have learned through trouble and trials that God's way is the very best way. He can see better than any of us can, and He knows a lot more than we do. Why not relax and let Him do the driving? Doesn't it make much more sense to have the Creator of this universe and the Lord of our lives order our footsteps and direct our paths?

Always on the other side of tribulation and adversity is a

wonderful place in God. It is a place of peace that comes from watching God take care of what is important to you. After you've developed a résumé with God, nobody has to tell you what a mighty God you serve. You realize it for yourself.

Over and over, I've watched God pull strings, open doors, shut doors, and simply make my existence wonderful on this earth. Only God can do that. Technically, we don't have to worry about even the minutest details of our lives.

Trust is what we come to from walking with God. After a while, even the least discerning person has to recognize the pattern of God's goodness. You learn to see the difference in your life from trusting Him. You realize it is so much better to lean on His strong arms and let Him help you through this journey.

When I glance over my shoulder to see how far He has brought me, I am glad for my journey with Him. The richness of our personal times together and the wealth of knowledge that He infused into my spirit bring me great joy. I have felt His blessing and favor. No, I wouldn't want to go back through everything again, but I cannot deny that those experiences of suffering with Him made me stronger, wiser, and whole. They made me better.

LOOK AT HOW GOOD YOU'VE GOT IT!

He has formed you, Trophy Woman, through many storms, and His plan is to get you safely Home to glory. You are a well-kept woman of God. Women who are well kept learn not to worry. Because you've been through so much, you are

His example. You are God's trophy, modeling His goodness and faithfulness. You are His handiwork that He shows off in heaven for all to look upon.

> YOU ARE HIS HANDIWORK THAT HE SHOWS OFF IN
> HEAVEN FOR ALL TO LOOK UPON.

Do you realize how well taken care of you are? Do you see His hand of mercy providing for you and His tender love sweeping sweetly over your life? Look at the countless ways He blesses you. God can be so good to you that you cannot share everything that He does. He can bless you so much that you get ashamed. God can and will take such good care of you that you can't help but be a blessing to others.

Has He given you so many clothes that you have to give some away? Has he given you cars, houses, and land? He can do these things, and sometimes He will. He can make your soul so happy and your life so peaceful, you have no other choice but to smile at strangers and bless those who offend you. You remember how good you felt when you first fell in love? Well, God cares for you so well that you can be too happy and too much in love to be hateful and bitter.

Has He kept you out of the doctor's office? Has He kept you from diseases for which you were at risk? How many times has He sent you an encouraging word when you were on the brink of despair? Take a look at the events that seemed disastrous in your life only to become some of the prime blessings of your life.

I knew a lady who gave birth to a child at a time when she should have been retiring from the workforce and finished with family rearing. Then, soon after her son was born, her husband died, leaving her an aging widow with a tiny baby. Many years later, when her son was a young adult, he cared for his old mother, picking up her prescriptions and looking in on her to see she had everything she needed. The very thing that seemed unfortunate turned out to bless her life and to bring her great joy as an elderly woman.

You don't really think it is coincidental that you've received beauty for ashes, do you? What I am trying to get you to understand is that nothing can harm you or hurt you permanently when you belong to Him. All that pertains to you is His principal concern.

READY TO SERVE

Listen, lady, you have learned too much about God to misunderstand Him. He has revealed Himself to you through your adverse circumstances and extreme ordeals.

We read in Isaiah of Jesus: "Butter and honey shall he eat, that he may know to refuse the evil, and choose the good" (7:15 KJV). God calls us to refuse the evil and choose good too. All that we have endured has helped us to know how to walk, making good and wise choices. Everything you've gone through helps you to make a difference in the lives of others.

There is nothing quite like the experience of suffering to give you compassion for others. You become keenly aware when

painful struggle has made your sister weary. You find it nearly impossible to resist having compassion on her and wishing her well, praying for her and making yourself available to her.

Christianity is not just about faith and believing. It also involves action: faith and works together. Performing the golden rule makes us golden girls—trophies—rare and precious. Too few will perform a deed or fulfill a need for others. It takes others-mindedness and unselfishness to give service on this level.

Doing something for someone else is an expression of faith that lifts. Other people matter! Women who realize that life is made up of more than themselves shine.

> WOMEN WHO REALIZE THAT LIFE IS MADE UP
> OF MORE THAN THEMSELVES SHINE.

It is wonderful to pray that our neighbor is blessed; it is better to *be* a blessing to her. It is stunning to witness someone who is not selfish and who understands the power of doing. Taking action to perform what you know another person wants and needs is wonderful for everyone involved. You have been blessed to be a blessing.

A FINAL WORD

I read somewhere recently that we have an average of thirty thousand hours to live. I guess that figure is based on a seventy- to seventy-three-year life span. We all know, though, that life deals so much out that it is easy to lose track of the time. After all, who's counting? We are severely distracted.

Jesus said to stay alert:

> No one knows about that day or hour [of Jesus' return], not even the angels in heaven, nor the Son, but only the Father. Be on guard! Be alert! You do not know when that time will come. It's like a man going away: He leaves his house and puts his servants in charge, each with his assigned task, and tells the one at the door to keep watch.
>
> Therefore keep watch because you do not know when the owner of the house will come back— whether in the evening, or at midnight, or when the rooster crows, or at dawn. If he comes suddenly, do not let him find you sleeping. What I say to you, I say to everyone: "Watch!" (Mark 13:32–37)

We are forewarned to be aware of the times. Often we think of time as it relates to the end of the age. But it is our day-to-day activities that matter most. What about the time God has personally allotted into our individual accounts? How we spend it is of the utmost importance.

The best way to ensure that we are getting a good deal out of life is to make each day count. Like finances, time is placed in your hands to do with as you will. What you do today will show up in your life tomorrow. Fill today with as much good as possible.

Everything you have gone through and continue to go through shapes your life and fashions you to guide someone else through this world. The fact that you have been well kept empowers you to help "keep" others—you can be a part of God's provision for them. Share what helped you endure the trophy-making process. Strengthen your sister to survive the flames as you have.

Trophies are made for showing, for celebrating, for shining. Trophy Woman, do all of those things!

TROPHIES ARE MADE FOR SHOWING,

FOR CELEBRATING, FOR SHINING.

Woman of God, don't wait to realize who you are in God. You are the prize! Jump up now, get to a mirror, and see yourself as one of God's Trophy Women! Go and look now! See!

Walking into Ready

Like stepping off a precipice
Without notice
Without warning
I have come out of a wilderness
Of confusion mingled with
Fumbled meanderings.

And
Like a floating feather
I slow-dance into a
Technicolor Kingdom filled with
Highways paved with
Radiant solidity,
Unequaled acceptance
And
Unimagined grace.

Questions for Reflection

❦ *Have you known a Trophy Woman like Jacqueline's mother? How was God's care for her apparent?*

❦ *"Have you noticed that God treats you better than you treat yourself?" How can you begin to honor yourself more?*

❦ *Do you believe you are "at your best and highest" during adversity, or after it? Why?*

❦ *Have you ever known an "odious woman"? What caused the woman's bitterness? Did she ever recover from it? (Have you been an odious woman?)*

❦ *Rather than praying that someone be blessed, how can you be a blessing for her today?*

Prayer

Lord,

I thank You for putting my sister in a place where she is secure in You. No, every little thing is not perfect in her life, but she has come to a place where that no longer matters. Lord, You have been so good to place her in a garden of life. Yes, she is sometimes confronted with difficulties even now, but they do not affect her in the same way. She is so secure in You. She loves this soft place in You, God. She is a rich woman. She is blessed beyond measure. She has arrived in a wealthy land by way of adversity. Her journey with You has led her into a lush and thriving field.

Father, teach her that on the other side of every struggle— no matter how long—is a river of peace and a place of serenity. Thank You for allowing her to see Your goodness in the land of the living. Thank You for allowing her to personally witness your gallant and fearless entry into her dark places. I love You for Your kindness to her. I love You for making all things beautiful in Your time. There is none like You.

In our lives we watch Your exceeding greatness. We are amazed at Your limitless graciousness unto us. Bless my sister reading this book to know firsthand Your unparalleled

power and richness. Let her know in the recesses of her being that she is neither a bruised rose, nor a forsaken flower, but open her eyes to see that she is the lily in her valley and the rose among the thorns. Let her know that, in spite of the odds, the challenges, the pain, she is a gift of light that You have allowed to come into this dark world. Bless her to be a blessing to others and let this woman know, Father, that she is the prize. Remind her that within her You've hidden treasures.

Lord, I praise Your name for making Your women to know that they are trophies par excellence lining the curio of heaven, handpicked to do Your work and to perform Your will. They are the prizes raised high in the air as symbols of victories wrought in their lives. Glory to You, Lord.

In Jesus' name we pray, amen.

NOTES

INTRODUCTION
1. *Merriam-Webster's Collegiate Dictionary*, 11th ed.
(Springfield, Mass.: Merriam-Webster, 2003), 1341.
2. John Newton, "Amazing Grace," public domain.

CHAPTER 2: THE WORK OF AN ARTIST
1. *Merriam-Webster's*, 383.

CHAPTER 6: THE TREASURES OF DARKNESS
1. *Merriam-Webster's*, 1332.

CHAPTER 7: SPOTS, WRINKLES, AND BLEMISHES
CAN TARNISH TROPHIES
1. *Merriam-Webster's*, 388.